# Praise for *Lenn*

"This is the most unique, fun, juicy
book I have read. (And I have read many.) It genuinely ~~
an interview with John Lennon in his highest expression.

The wisdom he shares comes with the same blend of
compassion and fervor as his artistic genius. It is as relevant to
our current global climate as it is timeless and priceless.

Ms. Ryan  expertly asks questions that call forth his insights
on everything from manifestation, education, social justice,
climate change, and money. There are also many personal
details shared about his life on Earth.

Run, don't walk, to read this book. A fast read, and a wise
investment in elevating your vibration and gaining a broader
perspective so needed at this time.

Thank you, Caroline Oceana Ryan, for this precious gem!"

> - Demetria Manuselis, Host of the Soul Freedom series
>   and Founder, AbundanceAngel.org

"Caroline Oceana Ryan has truly found the real John Lennon!

She has transcended the earthly plane to give us the voice
of Lennon's spirit, in order for him to speak his wisdom and
truth.

You will be captivated and amazed at the clear channel, which
transcends time!"

> - Shirley Bolstok, Medium, Metaphysical Worker, and
>   Author

"I'm sure many of us during this challenging time have wondered how our icons would have reacted, and how we would have greatly benefitted from their words of wisdom and grace.

Ms. Ryan's beautiful channeling offers this opportunity, as John Lennon speaks to us directly on many matters—including our friends the ETs, the heart-mind, and that 'the world's ills can't cost you your own life energies.'

In addition to the wise guidance, the energy that emanates from the pages is a powerful meditation in itself."

- Phil Hunter, English Language Lecturer, UK


"Deeply resonant and affirming, offering the gift of hope and a way forward in seemingly despairing times. Thank you, both!"

- Beatrice J, Musician, Canada


"Caroline Oceana Ryan brings John Lennon's essence through brilliantly!

I felt he was right there in front of me, sharing his words of enlightenment on being response-able in these challenging times."

- Rev. Jessica Hebert, Shaman and Teacher, BlueStarGaia.com


"John is right alongside Lord Michael and the Legions upon Legions of Galactic Forces that are here to see it through to this Sat Yuga—the Aquarian Age!

I met John & Yoko at the Troubadour in Hollywood in '68. I was only 14, yet I knew this was One of the Living Masters on the planet. Still IS! Sat Nam!"

- Rama Arjuna, RainbowRoundtable.net

"*Lennon Speaks* is a down to earth 'interview' with the man we all knew who started a revolution. To hear of his idea now of the kind of revolution he is part of, is something out of this world.

This is not an airy-fairy kind of interview. It is a deep spiritual conversation between a human being and a being of Light, sharing the whole story of what it was like to be on Earth and then venture into the heavens.

All I am saying is give this book a read, and soon everybody is going to be talking about it."

    - Ron M, Energy Healer, Thailand


"This book is golden! John Lennon is present once more with the energy and forthrightness we recognize from his time amongst us 40 years ago.

John never stopped seeking understanding. His choice of Caroline Oceana Ryan as his channeler has given us a very readable, thoughtful, insightful access to an expansive range of ideas and wisdom we can return to again and again.

In this conversation, Lennon speaks openly of his life as a Beatle and a person living in a rapidly changing era—one who was part of that impetus to change.

We are now in the vortex of that change! Lennon's voice once more adds clarity, and a depth of background supportive of our current experience."

    - Penny C C, Lightworker and Researcher

"*Lennon Speaks* perfectly captures the many complexities of John's personality, both in human and soul form.

Through Ms. Ryan's gifted ability to bring his spirit through so clearly, we once again receive his insight, candor, and timely advice for current day Earth living.

John Lennon's work for peace and humanity continues on through Ms. Ryan's work."

   - Sherri Be, Creative and Intuitive Coach


"Delightful and engaging . . . I could truly feel John's presence. I highly recommend this book."

   - Dr Vinayak, Doctor of BioEnergetics, Spiritual Coach, Channel, and Co-host of *A Night at the Roundtable*, BBSRadio.com


"This book is so full of authenticity and wisdom, and brings forth waves of musical memories as we visit with John Lennon through Caroline and the Collective's clear channeling, and Caroline's questions, which are both universal and personal.

Lennon responds sharing deep insights that both inspire our own healing path and our hopes for a future we can all embrace.

Thank you, Caroline, for being an impeccable messenger."

   - Carolyn Jones, Co-host, *Hard News on Friday* and *The True History Show*, BBSRadio.com

# Lennon Speaks

## Messages from the
## Spirit of John Lennon

**Caroline Oceana Ryan**

Ascension Times Publishing

# Dedication

*To the musicians, artists, and activists of the
Sixties and Seventies who changed the world with
their work and their vibration*

*To our Spirit teams of Angelic guardians, spirit guides
and higher self, the Archangels, and all the Angelic legions
constantly answering our calls for help
and encouragement*

*To those who paved the way into Ascendancy—
the Ascended Masters, who by gaining enlightenment and
developing their Lightbodies, encouraged all of us
to do the same*

*And to every Lightworker walking the Red Road to
higher consciousness*

*My profound thanks, Love, and respect for all you are
and all you do, at every moment.*

# Acknowledgments

My grateful thanks to early readers and reviewers of this book for their invaluable insights and support, and to my gifted graphic designer Jen McCleary.

My huge thanks to John, Paul, George & Ringo, who came into the world as unusual and brilliant Lights, and who gave us so much as a band and as individuals. They helped Light the way to a new era that is now unfolding.

My heartfelt thanks to John himself, for being a guide and mentor these many years since I was quite young, encouraging me to push the envelope, and to look at things from a new and higher perspective.

To dream, to inwardly Know, to Imagine the world as it can be.

And to all readers of these words, and all those joining together now to create the cooperatives, communities, experiences, and fifth dimensional consciousness of the New Earth: I send my Love and complete appreciation.

I honor and support your path of Light, always.

# Table of Contents

# Introduction

One day in June 2018, my friend Shirley Bolstok, a psychic medium and energy worker, mentioned to me at a gathering where we were both speaking, "John wants to work with you."

An accomplished channeler, Shirley has channeled John Lennon and other well-known musicians and historical figures for a while now. I had just finished channeling the Collective at the Hope Interfaith Center, a warm, enlightened spiritual community placed peacefully within a leafy suburb of Mankato, Minnesota.

The Collective are a group of Angels, Archangels, galactics, and other higher beings, and are the only beings I've channeled for a long time. I felt a little unsure about channeling John Lennon words and energies. He's a powerful spirit, and I wasn't sure I was the right one for the job.

I was nineteen when a friend phoned me from New York City on a December morning in 1980 to tell me that John had been shot and killed outside his home in Manhattan.

Like millions of others, I was shocked and grief-stricken. It felt impossible that yet another great leader of the Sixties—a gifted artist and Peace activist—would be stolen from us. The idea that we were meant to keep ourselves inspired to continue the work of Peace in the world without this visionary who had championed so much of it was hard to take.

So many creative people of my generation, whether poets or artists, musicians or activists, have found John's work irreplaceable. He was someone who made us feel less alone in the world, and helped us feel heard and encouraged in our experiences and realizations about life.

When Shirley told me that he had been one of my guides for a long time (as he is for so many), I felt honored. And comforted to know that those we look up to who are no longer in the physical are not so far away as we've been led to believe.

I put the idea of channeling John on a back burner for a while. I didn't anchor it into real action till summer 2019, when I channeled the majority of this book. That which was channeled in 2020 addresses a few situations that that tumultuous year gifted us with.

I say "gifted" because though there doesn't appear to be anything special or good about a global pandemic, raging wildfires, extreme weather, an economic depression, or political chaos, there is no denying that we are an Ascending planet, and that the Light pouring onto the Earth now is affecting every form of life on our planet.

Over and over, we are being asked to become our authentic selves, our higher selves, leaving behind all passivity, victimhood, smallness, and the third dimensional love of drama, and the shadows of the psyche.

Those processes can be taxing, painful, and many days, make no sense to us.

And so I offer you this book, my fellow traveler, as a support to your path, and I thank you for being brave enough to be on the planet at this time, to fulfill whatever beautiful vision you had in your own endless co-Creative dreams, while still in the higher realms.

We are here to make a real and positive difference, is what John would tell us. Except that now that difference is made etherically, as we anchor the energies of a whole higher dimension into human life and into the Earth Herself.

As you read this book or portions of it, if you are familiar with the Collective's work, you may well sense their presence and energies in it. I asked John about this, as I was sensing their presence during the channeling process, and he confirmed that he does work with them, and that they are working energetically through this book, contributing their energies to his.

And so—you are reading and receiving the Collective's input here as well, though the energies and presence I feel in these chapters is powerfully John's, and I am very thankful for that.

Each chapter begins with me asking a question, which John then answers or uses as a springboard for a related topic. The sentences in bold and italics are me responding and asking further questions.

You might object to John's voice here as not sounding very Liverpudlian, and he explains all that. Most of us have had many Earth lives. His life as a rock musician from the North of England was only one of them. Though it's the one we know him by, he is not fully encapsulated by that. Yet I am thankful he chose to come in and live as he did in that life, out on that leading edge.

I am also very thankful that so many on the red road to enlightenment are present on the Earth at this time! The Light I see now, in Light Bearers round the world, astounds and inspires me every day.

As with everything I channel, I ask that you take only that which resonates as being true for your path, and leave the rest.

This comes with many blessings for your path.

# 1

# Meeting John

*Namaste, Mr. Lennon! I've looked up to you since I was very small. I became a Peace activist after being influenced by your generation, your music, your inner journey, and your outer journey of taking a powerful stand for Peace in the world and equality for all people.*

*A psychic friend who channels you relayed the message that you want to work with me. She's told me that you've been a guide to me for some time. And that I've known you in other lives. All of that astounded me a bit.*

*But now that we're here, how can I assist? I know you have things to share. And I suspect you're a guide to many on the Earth now.*

I see you're preferring to be formal, maybe because of my "celebrity status" as people call it during their Earth lives.

Where I am now, no one has any kind of "status" so much as roles and particular frequencies that they radiate. So do call me

John, and I can call you Caroline, and we'll be on equal footing, as all persons are anyway.

Having seen your Light for a while now, I will say that like me, you have come up through the fires that Earth experience offers—in this life and many others—and managed to keep going. Many would have taken an alternate route, whether to escape the pain or to cut out of Earth life altogether.

As your Collective[1] would say, "that is understandable," but it was not your path to end your life or to live in ongoing avoidance of it. So you took the third choice, which is to tunnel through the obstacles as they were presented to you.

I'm aware that you still think of me as a Liverpudlian, and even expect me to still speak like one, which I can understand, as that's the only Earth life you consciously associate me with. In fact I have spoken many languages and dialects, including the ones that are pure sound and Light frequency, which so many are becoming more familiar with now.

You could as easily expect me to sound mid-sixteenth century French or seventeenth century German, or third century Chinese, if you wanted my voice to resemble what it was in an Earth life.

None of us are encapsulated or defined by Earth life "identities," which only really exist in our minds. Cultures assign certain meanings to certain ideas or labels, then people line up under those labels, and say, "This is what I am," or worse, "this is *who* I am."

### What we tried to do, the Beatles and I, then Yoko and I, was to assist people in no longer falling for hypnosis and entrainment.

Of course, intuitively, people know better, but they're powerfully brainwashed throughout life to avoid the truth of the matter. Which is that no one Earth culture or group can fully define anyone. It can try, but it fails every time.

---

[1] John refers here to a group of Angels, Archangels, Ascended Masters, and other higher vibrational beings who call themselves the Collective, "for we speak as One."

I work with many here in what you call the higher realms (some just call it Home) to assist those breaking out of that old mold, and realizing there are no definitive boundaries that outline who or what we are. That is an illusion now fading out of human consciousness, and high time it did.

What we tried to do, the Beatles and I, then Yoko and I, was to assist people in no longer falling for the hypnosis and entrainment. To stand on their own and to think for themselves and to realize when they were being lied to.

And to wake up from it ourselves.

I was able to come across with these ideas far more clearly and succinctly while working with Yoko than with my three friends and brothers, because she and I were not under the ridiculously narrow constraints of having to please the music industry. We just did what we knew to be important, and let the chips fall where they may.

We didn't feel it was up to us to regulate people's reactions to us—their approvals or disapprovals. We were going to carry on, regardless.

That was one of the reasons we stepped out of bounds so often. We wanted people to see what was possible. And that neither of us would disappear in a puff of smoke immediately after a particular performance or after a particular recording came out, just because we had broken the rules about what was acceptable or expected.

So we'll carry on with that in the next chapter . . .

# 2

# Walking Around Hypnotized

*I agree that the human race is in a state of hypnosis and entrainment. A lot of people feel that way. Can you clarify what you mean when you say that?*

*And would you say that's true of every person and every culture in the world?*

Human beings have been in a state of hypnosis and illusion for thousands of years. Yes, it affects nearly every person and culture, to varying degrees.

I used to get visions of this in my last life, and not just when taking hallucinogens. They would come to me in dreams, in meditations, in sudden images. They were messages sent me to assist in the awakening of the race, which happens to a lot of artists.

Plenty of people get those images and downloads, though a lot of it is repressed. I never doubted those messages. Because in those moments, I understood my own life and that of many others, more clearly than I ever had.

What I saw, was that people believe they're awake and aware, and are being told the truth about life on their planet.

What's transpired over the millennia. Who's been in charge, and how. When in fact, they have been solidly lied to for longer than most can imagine.

I'm not speaking of politics or religion, which are just levers and tools used to manipulate the human race. This goes a lot deeper than that. It has to do with the intention and disposition, you might say, of certain races of people whom you call "ETs" (though we're all that, if we trace our lineage). And it has to do with the history of this Universe, which stretches beyond what you could calculate in Earth years.

Earth was long ago invaded and colonized by several groups of beings. Some call one of these races reptilians, others simply call them "invaders," because they not only came in unannounced (nearly everyone does). They set up power structures that enslaved anyone who was not of their culture.

I use the generic term "invader" because specific names and cultural associations are not particularly helpful. That's one of the bigger traps, in fact. Even spiritually aware, highly conscious people are capable of falling into the "Us and Them"—the separatism that false Earth systems have run on for millennia.

*If they can keep you fighting one another, convinced that you are facing down the Other—the shadow aspect of your own psyche, and of the spiritual realm—then they have you trapped in what many call duality. And duality has been the lowest trap of all.*

## There is what Eckhart Tolle calls "the good that has no opposite." But you don't get there through duality.

You may feel that the worst things are the things that are physically played out: human trafficking, war, the pandemic, drug trafficking by government agencies, exploitative corporations, the wealthiest individuals. Yes, all of that is very dense. But those things themselves are not strictly to blame.

Look at the machinery behind it. Look at the wheels that turn to make all that density possible.

Again, I'm not talking strictly about politics or religion. Allow those misguided expressions to be the foolish enterprises they are! Don't stress over them. And don't feel either of them is what you are "fighting" or will be saved by. In fact, come out of the fight. Fighting was created by Duality.

If you live in duality, then there's always a winner and a loser. There's always Light and Dark. There's always a good man and a bad one, a good woman and a bad one. There are always races that are "naturally" good and pure, and ones that are "naturally" low and ignorant. Same with cultures, ideas, emotions, ways of speaking. Even table manners.

Under the stiff reign of Duality, there are always religions that worship the wrong god, or that worship the right god in the wrong way. Constant judgments. And in the end, no one wins. Because you cannot walk the thin line between Dark and Light forever. Sooner or later, you fall off that very thin bridge into the cold water below, into moments you were never trained for.

Suddenly, you're a part of that other world, and finding it not foreign. You're seeing there's some darkness in the Light, and some Light in the darkness of every human expression. And yes, there is what the author Eckhart Tolle calls "the good that has no opposite"—yes, that does indeed exist.

But you don't get there through duality.

*OK, I follow. The yin/yang symbol demonstrates the idea that there's a bit of darkness in the Light and a bit of Light in the darkness.*

*But some people believe we set up duality on this planet as a kind of experiment. We decided we would allow the shadow aspect, the lower realms and our own lower tendencies, to influence and be a big part of Earth life, and that we'd learn something from that.*

And human beings *have* learned from it! A lot of in-depth growth in those experiences. They also learned it can all go way too far. It's not just a lab experiment or research anymore, where you try on different shapes and colors. It's been a nightmare gone out of control.

Humanity and the Earth have chosen now to leave duality, and that is a great relief to all who saw Earth's and humanity's very existence hanging in the balance for a while. Some trace of human life would have survived even a mass extinction event. But what is to be gained from that, when it's already happened in other eras? Nothing.

On this particular timeline, as chosen by the mass of humanity, Earth will survive. Humanity will survive.

And then everyone will have to learn not to think in terms of Dark and Light opposing one another, living in eternal judgment of one another.

Of course, it isn't easy to go through life not making judgments. I tried—we all tried, and we usually failed. The older generations made fun of us in the Sixties and Seventies, as we were using phrases like "follow your own path" or "do your own thing" to allow people room to wake up and realize first their own individual consciousness, then the interconnection of all peoples, all consciousness. To the older folk, questioning the norm was not only foolish and self-destructive. They thought it showed complete lack of gratitude for all they'd given us.

In fact, what we'd been given was often little more than a humiliating, just-getting-by, conform-or-you'll-pay-dearly-for-your-rebellion existence that is clearly visible in so many countries.

What upsets the power structure in the United States, regarding everyone earning a living wage and receiving socialized benefits, isn't anything to do with "socialism." The elites argue against allowing benefits and fair pay because they don't want everyone getting by to the degree that you still have your dignity and your individual choices. That's too empowering.

They also don't want people living long enough to figure out who's really in charge and why. And they most definitely don't want people seeing one another as equals. That's why the meritocracy, the "earn your way by working hard" belief is there, though the rule-makers themselves don't actually live by that, as so many of them are born into big money.

The reason I bring up the idea of releasing the need to judge others (people, ideas, cultures) is that it's one of the hardest things a human being could ever do. As I say, I didn't make it on that front. Almost no one does. Obviously, I didn't Ascend while in a human body.

I loved the ego aspect of my personality—there was too much there I didn't want to give up. Even when it was killing me at one point, during the time that my addictions and unhealed "core wounding" were threatening to swallow me whole. I thought I'd lose my edge as an artist if I gave that up.

And if you've clung a long time to one lifeline, it's the only thing you know. It can feel too risky to move to another.

So that when I left Earth I did so a very faulty, yet somewhat wiser man than when I enjoyed the height of fame and popular approval. It amazes me now, though it didn't then, that so many think that being well-known will justify their existence not only to thousands or millions of people, but to themselves. Far from it.

It will push you to call into question everything you have ever called real or normal. Suddenly none of the old clothes fit, you might say. None of the old voices of reassurance ring in your ear as they once did. Even old friends seem strange and remote and almost irrelevant at times, unless they're going through the same thing.

It solves nothing. It opens the door to many more questions and complications than you could imagine. That's true for most, and it was for me.

Again—this is because we are born already partly asleep. And it's the job of what is called "society" to ensure that we go *completely* to sleep, utterly under hypnosis and control by sound, image, and vibration, by the age of seven or eight. Of course some never do. And so most Earth cultures are set up to ostracize and ridicule those who remain clear on who they are and what is happening around them.

Actions are taken to ensure that even some of these are properly aligned with the higher agenda. And so there are communes, monasteries, universities, "alternative communities" that thrive in believing they have chosen a higher way, when in most instances, they are simply an interesting variety on the hierarchical deception everyone else bows down to.

Is there a way out? A way to recall who you are and why you're here? To step out of the struggle and dislike of being human, and allow the greater current of the Universe to take you on the ride of your life?

That's what we're here to talk about. So stay tuned, as they say on American TV . . . .

# 3

# Emotion and Where It Gets You

*Can you tell us how they keep us asleep, and why?*

You know all about it. Everyone does. You fall in line because you receive so many threats, so many "programming" moments as a small child that you come to understand very quickly that if you want a roof over your head and food to eat, you must bow to "the authorities."

You saw early on that it was a dangerous game to step out on your own, to question the programming. Maybe some of that would be tolerated in those "rebellious teen years" as everyone loves calling them. But once you hit your late teens or early twenties—time's up! Time to conform and get serious. Don't make us ashamed! Get a job, or get an education and then a job. And do as you're told in those places, just as you had to throughout your upbringing.

Of course, there's always this feeling amongst those who see through the veil that once you earn a certain amount, get to a certain point in your work, or save a particular sum, you'll buy your freedom. You'll work creatively or travel the world or volunteer to work with "those less fortunate."

And yes, some actually do this. Many have done this. Yet in Western culture, it is difficult to maintain a highly simplified life without strong commitment. You've been taught to be ashamed of that—how pathetic, that you don't own very much! So sooner or later most will fall in line, because even the ground you walk on has been ingrained with the "earn a living and prove yourself by what you buy" pressure.

What a bizarre idea! As if you aren't qualified to breathe without having earned it first. Rubbish!

But to answer your question, let's get back to our friends the ETs . . .

\* \* \* \* \* \*

Thousands of years ago on this planet, life was the idyllic version of Earth that some artists have tried to recreate. Colors were more vivid, sound was harmonious. Food was clean and healthy, water was crystalline pure.

Technologies were used every day that Earth beings tend to only dream of now, such as space travel for your average person, and healing with sound and Light and color. Anything needed was created with thought—a focus held by individuals or groups. People spoke to each other and the animals, trees, plants, and Earth's elemental spirits via Light language or a telepathic energy exchange.

If there was disagreement, it was solved by focusing on a common aim. Both parties would work with the intention of what each wanted to create, until both intentions resonated at the same level, so that agreement could be reached on what was going to be created. This is what you now call "energy work." But at that time, it was simply everyday life.

No one died from illness or "old age." They lived for thousands of years, and left the planet for one destination or another when they felt the time was right for that.

There was no money exchanged, because all that was needed was readily available. No governments ran as they do now, permitting only certain people from certain families to rule, while money and favors are exchanged for outer power. Though some in "places of power" are honest now, they are few and far between, and often greatly endangered by the power brokers pressuring them to conform.

The bribery, threats, and control that have long occurred behind closed doors were not the norm then. It was a transparent system, and a fair and equal one. Representatives were chosen for their spiritual advancement and desire to serve.

All buildings were built with respect for Earth's requirements and well-being, and no one interfered with this. No trees were destroyed wantonly, no oil or coal extracted, no air or water or soil polluted.

You get the idea—the planet held civilizations that were advanced in every respect.

Then the invaders came. Some had already been on Earth for a while, allowing it its idyllic status. Then they made the Earth-changing decision to infiltrate the systems they saw around them. They maneuvered their thinking and preferences so as to engage and intertwine them with the thinking and systems around them.

This took several hundred years—not a long time, to them. They knew their system had worked on other planets, and would work on this one, as most on Earth were unsuspecting of the nature of invader interests. Or foolishly believed their system to be so strong that "it could never happen here." Yet it did.

And so there were those who were presumed to be friends to the Earth, who shapeshifted into attractive appearances as needed. They came to befriend and then manipulate leaders and healers, temple priests and priestesses, animals, everyday humans. Few suspected their true nature and interest—people had been taught to expect the best and only see the best in all.

So over time, as their low intentions won out over the high intentions of those around them, the creeping darkness appeared to overcome the Light.

They brought in Duality. They brought in fear and distrust and discord. They brought in suspicion and self-centeredness and self-protection. They brought in the idea of a hierarchy in which some beings were naturally superior to those who were naturally inferior. They brought all that in, and more.

In time, Earth was given to wars, to exploitation of her beautiful gifts and abundance, to exploitation of people and animals, and the twisting of ideas of who or what a god is, and what he or she exacts of mere mortals.

These situations were created as a form of control over Earth's populations. Not only human populations, but also animals, plants, trees, water, air, soil. Everything had to come under the enslavement and imprisonment of the prevailing power structure.

### We are, even in those sleep-filled moments, still reaching back in our memory to Atlantis or Lemuria, remembering who we were.

Whereas people had been able to have lives that stretched out over hundreds, even thousands of years on the Earth, they now faced increasing levels of illness and early physical death. They faced the energetic scarring and soul imprints of trauma, degradation, and shock. And they faced the narrowing of what are now called psychic or spiritual abilities, via a loss of DNA strands—an intentional deactivation of human DNA, down to the double-strand DNA most people have had for thousands of years.

This lowered human consciousness to where fear was our natural state. And when in fear, people will take the hand of nearly anyone offering them safety.

Modern life has offered a panoply of control mechanisms to ensure human beings almost never think for themselves. Even in some of the world's poorest villages, makeshift dwellings will have television, video, digital gaming, popular music. The power brokers have intentionally created many powerful inroads to capturing people's inner frequency and tuning it to the vibration they prefer.

So much so, that you've only ever had a few thoughts in your entire life that were truly your own. That is so for everyone. And that's not even touching on the control of education, religion, cultural norms. Or the vibrations of fear and chaos continuously beamed out across the planet by powerful technologies.

Now, the interesting thing about human beings, is that we never completely forgot.

One of the reasons we don't fight against the hypnosis or brainwashing heaped upon us from the cradle, is that we are, even in those sleep-filled moments, still reaching back in our memory to Atlantis or Lemuria or similar civilizations. We're remembering who we were. And that is not a "fight" frequency. It's an Allowing the Flow frequency.

Nearly all who are on the planet now had at least one life on one of those beautiful continents, or in other advanced civilizations. They are not "mythical." And all have a hidden longing that rises to the surface at times for the kind of beauty, tranquility, abundance, and joy we experienced in those lives, along with the honor of serving others.

So we allow the distractions—the constant need for digital devices or entertainment or gossip or desiring objects—because it's too painful to look around and see what Earth's people have lost. What humans have slowly yet willingly given up, for the false comfort of "safety and security."

Look at your current systems. You can see how that game is still being played.

Particularly in these days when the higher forms of Light reaching the planet are awakening nearly everyone to one degree or another, the Safety and Security card is still being played over and over. The controllers' names, faces, and cultural associations change over time, but not the message—that remains the same.

*You're not safe, so you'd better distrust / hate / go to war with / fear / cut away from this group or that / take this medication! Otherwise, we can't guarantee your safety . . .*

Of course there are always some who have awakened to the deception fully enough to see humanity has been played, to extremes.

### So what's different now, in this new era? Or are things on Earth as hopeless as they ever were?

They're not at all hopeless! That's the bizarre and brilliant part.

Because of this higher Light coming in now, not only from the Great Central Sun but from various star clusters and

13

astrological configurations—the energies are so empowering, that humanity is awakening its collective memory of what it is to be whole. To live in Peace and normalcy. To release the need to control and contort people's ideas and actions so that they conform to a system they never wanted.

Yes, humanity chose to allow Duality to come into Earth experience, to a good extent. And now, realizing this great experiment has gone too far, you are choosing to come out of it.

I can tell you, Earth's former overlords are none too pleased about that. They're doing all they can to stay in control via the old methods of shock and trauma, which they've used for thousands of years. Sometimes it's through weather and extremes in temperature or rain or snow. Sometimes it's Earth manipulation (earthquakes, volcanic eruptions, fires, floods, hurricanes). Or war, or mass shootings or fires, or outbreaks of illnesses. Or planning false cataclysmic events, such as a fake "alien invasion."

Yes, those have been tried. You may have read on the internet that the fake invasion was an idea someone wanted to carry out in recent times, and it has been stopped. But I can assure you, it's been done before, or variations of it.

### And people bowed down to these ETs as gods? Accepted their higher technologies, which had been hidden from public view, as magic or Divinity?

It was worse than that. They allowed themselves to be entrained vibrationally to where they were no longer full individuals. They gave up their independent thought and feeling, and allowed themselves to be energetically implanted so they would follow a program of servitude and slavery. And they were revised on a DNA level, so that they and all their descendants would accept unthinkingly all they were told by this group of "rulers" who seemed to have come straight from heaven.

A number of religions and political systems were begun this way, as well as forms of scientific control over human life that are utterly corrupt, and continue to this day. But they are ending now.

*You recount all this grim history with a disapproving tone, yet you don't seem to be angry. You seem pretty calm.*

*Should we who are still on Earth also not be angry? Should we be as objective as you and those in the higher realms are, yet somehow also do something about it?*

Well, the invaders are fascinated by the wide human emotional range, and also not susceptible to emotional ups and downs themselves. So in a way, you're streets ahead of where they are, in terms of understanding the depth of experience on this planet.

In another way, you're easily manipulated through your emotions, because humans take feelings so seriously, and find them so motivating. You speak and act on the sheer strength of what you're feeling at the moment.

I did this no end in my last Earth life. Emotions powered my music and my art. It powered my activism, and my love for the people in my life. It meant I had to protect and provide for them, which men usually feel they have to do for their partner and children. It meant, in the early days, that the other boys in the band had to be looked after, that we had to work as a cohesive unit. If one of us stood apart, that had to be answered, till the tear was mended.

It also meant that when I was falling apart, my relationships suffered badly, because there were times I had very little self-control, whether it was a matter of the women I was attracted to or thought I could own, or how I expressed myself when drunk or high or enraged, or inspired.

So there's a broad spectrum there, and you don't have to be an artist or an angry working class lad to express that range of emotion (though it helps).

These other beings who long ago appointed themselves Earth's rulers see that broad emotional range and figure, "Excellent! We'll launch this situation or that, and manipulate them through mass psychological trauma and emotional scarring. That's already been rooted in them from childhood experiences."

Or they'll step up the programs that are based on what they realized long ago: that human sexuality is one of the race's great driving forces. That people can be controlled through their sexuality if that control is blatant enough to direct a lot of their thinking, yet subtle enough that the control isn't noticed. It just gets called a personal preference. A personal preference for porn, or emotionally detached one-night stands, or abusive relationships, either as abuser or victim.

You've channeled from your friends the Collective about the Victim/Savior programming, which run rampant through human life. So say you're the combative type, and physically aggressive, because you were raised that way or trained in your youth to solve problems that way. If you're convinced that you're "right," and that someone else has tried to victimize you, you can then take the stand that you are completely justified in punching the daylights out of them.

On a bigger scale, that could be taken as reason to wage war against a particular group or a country.

Now, none of that is accidental. Your governments control whole groups of vulnerable people who have no inner home. No sense of self, other than the mind control programs they're subjected to.

*It's a lost soul format, using violence to solve something, whether you're talking about those who sit to the right or the left of any issue.*

*We all want to change the world. "But when you talk about destruction/Don't you know that you can count me out . . ."*

That lyric still stands, for both ends of the spectrum!

When you talk about doing something, raising awareness with tools such as books like these is one of the biggest things you can do. (Outside of music, of course!) Because those who truly wish to know the Light, who are seeking honesty and self-understanding and true wisdom, are going to wake up when they're ready, however big a shock it might be.

They're going to realize that the particular god, political party, or lifestyle they've been worshipping is a lie. That it was never what they were told it was. Not a part of their authentic selves. It's just a waystation on their soul journey, not the journey itself.

Should people be angry? Your guides have said many times, "Feel the pain or the anger if you need to. But don't live there. Release it and move on as soon as you can. Return to your center, your true self, who is always calm."

I agree. *Why give them a foothold? Why react to what they do and say, as if they determine the content and quality of your day?*

They've been traumatizing certain populations in quiet ways, and others in more obvious ways, and now it's gotten obvious everywhere. First they create the problem and lie about the cause, then they create the so-called solution. Meanwhile they're reaping dense energy all along the way.

So a particular population suffers from being displaced, vilified, or attacked in some way. The effect is not only that population's shock and upset. It extends to those who read or hear about it, and feel helpless to stop it.

It's a highly efficient system, and a huge reason why they've allowed humans to have first television and now the internet. Effective systems of mental entrainment, emotional exploitation, and mass programming.

They have rerouted what it means to be a human, over the millennia. Yet now you're changing it again.

## Image a distressed community releasing panic and reaction, and coming into Peace and calm.

You're coming back into your mastery, your individuality, your inner beauty. You're remembering the co-Creator abilities that are intrinsically yours, though you've been taught to avoid using them.

You're claiming that sovereignty you've been told for centuries is not yours to claim. So it's sat dormant for an age, an era of destruction that is now ending.

Your sovereignty, your freedom, has been waiting for this time to appear.

You're coming out of an age of destruction, the *kali yuga*. That doesn't really fit who you are anymore as a race or a planet. So maybe, instead of getting angry or despairing the next time you hear about one of their clever plans being enacted, decide what you *do* want for yourself and your family or community, or anyone's family or community. Instead of just dissolving into rage that only feeds their machinery anyway.

*One of the more powerful things you can do, is mentally image that distressed community or region releasing panic and reaction, and coming into Peace and calm.*

Moving through the obstacles before them as if they were annoyances more than devastating road blocks. Calling on the power of their own higher selves and all higher beings waiting to assist.

People get upset, because they feel that "heaven should intervene" in times of stress and shock, yet it doesn't. But these beautiful Beings of Light cannot assist until you call them in! Because you live in a free will zone. So expect them. Call on them. Envision all kinds of help coming in now, and give thanks for it.

Your expectations send out a vibration into the world of energy that molds that energy into outer events, far more powerfully than you could know. You create things this way all the time; you just haven't realized the power of it yet. Haven't fully harnessed it to get it consistently working for you, though I do see that unfolding.

Another powerful thing: asking your own higher self the best action for you to take. It might be contacting someone in government to insist on constructive action from them, or assisting or supporting a community group or nonprofit that's addressing the issue responsibly. When things happen in your own community, especially, that can be a call for your involvement in some way. That includes envisioning solutions and healing for all involved—one of the biggest things you can do.

Because you can't really hop on a plane every day and fix what's happening across the country, or around the world!

Running around trying to fix things, even if you have the resources for that, "would take your *whole day*." And keep in mind that each time they are about to return to live another Earth life, people write certain obstacles into their life plan, including traumatic events, to learn from them. To see how they show up inside of that.

Thankfully that sort of baptism by fire is no longer necessary for inner growth. You're living out the last of that old Earth paradigm that a tough time draws out the best in people.

Each person returns to the Earth for more growth and learning hundreds of times, sometimes thousands. So you can release your surprise that Earth is a tough place to be! You've seen it all before. Stop reacting.

Establish a place of Peace within yourself every morning, by concentrating purely on your breathing, or a spot on the wall, or the candle flame, or a blade of grass if you're sitting outside. Use a guided meditation if you prefer that. Go into a meditative, "inner quiet" space while practicing music, or practicing yoga.

Then, whatever happens outwardly, come out of reaction. Return to that quiet place of calm inside, as soon as possible.

That is your true self. Not the conditioned automaton, performing as programmed.

You've heard that phrase, "Be who you are," and this is what it means, in your time. Finally, *finally*—be your wide awake yet dreamer and inventor self, creating new worlds out of old ones, freedom out of captivity, wellness out of imbalance.

What else have you come here for?

# 4

# No Victims, No Saviors

*You've made clear we're here to be our true selves, and to overcome the mass programming. To wake up finally.*

*Yet how do we wake up from the manipulation, and from energy interferences of all kinds, when that's the only "us" we know?*

*The old power structure has infiltrated and is controlling so many "enlightenment" teachings—particular modes of thought, spiritual teachers, spiritual movements.*

*So we might think we're awake, when lo and behold, we've simply fallen for the old tricks in a new guise. Another form of programming and control.*

*Where's the awakening there?*

Actually, the whole human race is in an awakening process. It's just not obvious to everyone yet.

This is why there are so many strange and unhappy events occurring around the world at one time. All the unrest and disturbance is happening in such steep and extreme degrees because as I say, the old elite have never been more terrified in all their thousands of years upon the Earth.

This time, it's not a political movement motivating them to increase the fear quotient, to keep their control over hearts and minds. It's not even the astrological alignments, which point to renewal and reformation.

It's all of you who are terrifying them, with your energies and awareness! You're expanding and rising so exponentially that those in the higher realms can barely keep up with your progress!

What's awkward about the awakening process, is that most will realize they've been duped for centuries—brainwashed, manipulated, enslaved. So that upon awakening, they feel a very real anger coming up. That anger is rooted in every single Earth life they've ever lived, in which they witnessed injustices and inequalities. Most these they were either powerless to stop, or punished for even noticing.

The anger phase won't carry on indefinitely if you're willing to move out of it. And as we said earlier, I'd suggest moving out of it as soon as possible. Anger is a lower vibrational emotional frequency that pulls people down, even while it motivates them to speak up about things they feel shouldn't be happening. It's not the vibration from which much better, more equitable realities are built. It's just helpful in pointing out the madness of the current ones.

## The mind and the heart are finally meeting up again.

Don't waste your life energy on reaction. Let's move out of that, and into positive moments. Carry images of complete equality for all persons, a peaceful end to all violence, food and homes and medical care for everyone. Positive outcomes for all. Positive ways of living for all peoples.

Starting from that vision, we can move to the practical. How do we create communities where everyone is fed, housed, clothed, educated? Where their health needs are seen to in natural ways? Where their spiritual life is one of joy and adventure, not stiff rules?

How do we create nations where no one cultural viewpoint impinges on another?

That's what I envisioned on Earth. That's the sort of community I wanted to help build, or at least help others envision. Then when my second son was born, he became the central focus of my life. And I was moving then into a time of introspection and healing of old wounds from this and other lives. So my focus was taken off those areas for a while, and moved to the personal.

Then I began to realize there's no separation between the two. And that there's a bigger word—consciousness—that involves both.

***Is that the biggest part of our Awakening—the realization that we have to free ourselves first, you might say?***

I'd say it is, though many political activists would call that short-sighted and insufficient. They would prefer to see it all as a matter of outer action. Changing the system by shifting who is in what role, what laws are passed, what unjust laws are dissolved, seeing how many marches and petitions can be created.

All of that is brilliant and powerful. It's an expression of the kind of growth humans are going through now. Yet it's not the whole journey. It's an outer indication of what is happening in people's heart-minds, as you call them.

That's a great term, heart-minds. Because the mind and the heart are finally meeting up again. That's one very big reason why it's getting increasingly harder for politicians and religious leaders to pass laws and edicts that assist them in getting away with every crime in the book.

People are becoming increasingly aware of their own inner voice. And that's powerfully influencing and inspiring their outer voice. And as they speak up, they're giving notice to every part of the old power structure that this is not business as usual. Great change is happening that can't be stopped, by anyone.

*And yet you point to a list of ongoing crimes that are too many to mention, and seem to be getting worse! It's crazy, the things they're doing now, particularly to induce more fear, shock, and trauma in women and children. In families.*

*I know they use our denser emotional energy for their etheric power grid, and to keep our consciousness in the lower frequencies. Even our "moral outrage" about corruption they manage to use, in some ways.*

And yet, the outrage at their crimes wasn't planned by them. It's not their preference. They prefer a quiet, complacent crowd of sheep who react with shock, then look for safety, and unquestioningly do as they're told.

That's what they prefer. Not thousands or millions of people who are up in arms about the unchecked situations creating climate change and the toxins in food, soil, and water. People pouring onto the streets with placards and banners and chanting that change must come, that Black Lives Matter or that Native Lives Matter, or pointing to the real sources of illness, the toxicity of some vaccines. That is not their preference, though they do try to harness some of that emotion, yes.

Yet at base that emotion is powerfully interwoven with the Light coming to the planet right now. And I spell "Light" with a capital L, as you do, because you are correct that these are not unconscious photonic rays coming in, but highly conscious lifeforms assisting humanity in the biggest leap it's ever taken.

Who ever heard of a planet moving from the third to the fifth dimension? When third dimensional vibration is so low that it resonates with chaos, violence, general "lost"-ness and confusion? There are third dimensional planets that are less mad than this one, but they too suffer the results of living in so little higher Light and awareness. And now Earth stands to well surpass them as she moves up into the next higher dimension, which is the fifth. (In the fourth dimension, Time collapses into All Times, so that only Present Time exists. So the next move up for daily life is the fifth dimension, or fifth level density.)

This is why so many are celebrating now—more likely, those of us who are not in the madness of this astounding Ascension you're experiencing, which can be taxing and demanding many days.

### *Are you also in the Ascension process, even though you're in spirit?*

Of course I am. We all are. I'm still an Earth being, at least in part. Many are part Earthling and part other-worlds. Nearly all are a huge mix of DNA from this planet or that star, and sometimes, other Universes.

Soul origin is a fascinating thing. But you'll note that your friends the Collective are slow to give people labels regarding where they originated from. People raised in 3D will tend to take on cultural associations and alliances, and attach to them, in the ego-mind.

There's no progress to be had there! No different from saying, "I'm a Northerner, therefore I have these characteristics that are lower/higher or better/worse than you Southerners." That's all an ego construct. People tend to enjoy defining themselves with outer labels, and taking refuge in that. That's just more duality. More Us and Them.

### *How are you being affected by the Ascension process? And are you cheering on the process?*

I am cheering it on, but not with the lighthearted detachment of those who come from elsewhere. They watch from a distance. These are beings who haven't lived Earth lives, and are just sort of "parked" on or around the Earth as she evolves, to observe and learn. Those who have incarnated upon Earth for the first time volunteered to come forward and assist. (These are the ones you call Starseed, and there are many millions of them now.)

I'm involved in the Ascension process in my own way. I work with human consciousness still, through music, through visual art, through forms of theatre that exceed what most people think of as plays or performance. I work with those who on a higher level are willing to work with me, whose energies and intentions are aligned with freeing the planet, without the "rescue" component.

That is just not on. That is not freedom! That is replacing one regime with another. You will not get there by meekly worshipping yet another life form. What you seek is your own sovereignty, your own voice, your own right of way. No one can hand you that. Others can help support you in your journey, but not give you that, no.

*Yet we've been trained to constantly expect and ask for a savior! How do you get away from thousands of years of programming? It's in our DNA! Our very cells.*

Yes, absolutely. But you can still make powerful determinations inwardly, and hold points of focus that actually re-route your DNA.

That can happen. That's not science fiction.

*Are we that powerful? Because we've been trained to believe that we have to wait till a machine is invented to do these things before we can even slightly approach change in them.*

*The way people are taught to "wait" for a cure to cancer, for example, when natural cures for that have existed for thousands of years.*

Yes, you are that powerful. And yes, there is a cure to every illness and disorder on the planet, including those manufactured by your former "overlords."

Technology is fine in and of itself. It can do a great deal. But all it does, in the case of curing serious illness at its root, is raise the vibration of the patient to where that no longer resonates with the vibration of the illness. It can also awaken the body's cells to where they remember how to renew and revitalize themselves.

And it can lift certain unbalanced aspects of a person's thought and emotions, which are always reflected in the body, to where that imbalance doesn't exist in their reality.

It can do a lot. But technology is only a slight reflection of what you yourself can do once you move into a higher vibration, by your own sheer focus and expectation. And it's finite. You are not finite. Co-Creation—it's gone by different names over the eons, but that's as clear a name as any.

***What if even just one-third of the people in the world concentrated on Peace—disappearing all war, all human trafficking, all civil conflict and police violence, domestic violence, false imprisonment, hunger, the pandemic—for one full minute a day?***

***What if we envisioned all of that healed? Would anything change?***

In less than a month, the entire planet would transform. The Light coming in now would be assisting you in ways undreamed of in past centuries. Believe me—believe all of us who are in Spirit: You would create the kind of revolution that makes the old regime wake up at night screaming.

***Now I can hear people saying, "Is it that simple? Is it that easy?"***

It is that simple, but it's not that easy just yet. Because people have been taught that "just thinking something" doesn't have any real life-changing power, when in fact it has unending power. The power of Creation.

You can't go out and Do something, without first imaging yourself doing it. An idea is really a mental picture. That's your platform, your blank canvas. It's picking up the paintbrush and deciding what to paint. Without that initial moment—the conception before the birth—nothing happens.

This is why the whole idea of the Divine Feminine had to be squashed. Well, it was one reason it was crushed, and in horrible ways that would warn people away from it for as many Earth lives as possible. The Divine Feminine is the point of conception—the Originator and Design. The Inspiration. The spark of Life.

Without that coming into play, you can't jump up and go create something outwardly unless you want to just keep bumping into a wall or a corner and going nowhere all day long. You need somewhere to go to. There has to be a design first. Take that original power to conceive a vision away from people, and you turn them into robots, awaiting orders. And that's exactly what happened.

Emphasizing a warped masculinity as the true nature of God, and vilifying the Divine Feminine as weak, implausible, inherently wrong—it was all one. The one side of the coin wouldn't work without the other.

Conception is the start of everything. Yes, you live in what people call a physical world. Yet the whole operation still spins on energy formation. So that sometimes just holding an idea in your mind, especially if you back it with very positive emotion, is all it takes to literally draw that situation into your life—without your having done much of anything outwardly.

That creation ability exists within you. *You* are the point of conception, the idea originator. What is called "just your imagination" is far, far more than that. It's a world-maker. A planet-changer.

And don't they know it, friends.

**This is another reason why the powers-that-were robbed us of so much of our natural human DNA—to ensure that our minds could only do and realize and envision so much?**

That and other gifts. Telepathy and transmutation, teleportation and telekinetic abilities, and many others. Healing or creating via projected thought or image. Those tend to collapse without those DNA strands. Or they take tremendous effort to generate within the consciousness. And then what?

You can shift your vibrational density to where you can walk through a wall—wow, congrats. Does that feed hungry children? Does that speed along the evolving of your spirit? Does that heal or enliven you or others? Not necessarily. It's just impressive.

So the ability in and of itself is not the point. The higher consciousness that should naturally accompany it is the point.

*Please tell me you believe that we are getting there. That you can see, from where you are, that we are moving into higher consciousness. That we are coming into a time when we realize that Love is all that matters, and the only reason we're here.*

What's happening hasn't yet occurred to everyone consciously, but a slight majority of the human race are experiencing that evolution, yes, and that is a great moment. Everyone is shifting in relation to the powerful higher Light coming into the planet right now. Believe it or not, *even 10 percent of the human race choosing Love, choosing Peace over the usual madness, would be enough to change everything.*

We're seeing a far greater shift than that!

*Thank you, my friend—I am greatly relieved to hear that. So these really are Ascension times we live in?*

Of course. Why else would you all be here now?

# 5

# Music as a Portal

*Would you talk to us about your life as a musician?*
*Did you choose music, or did music choose you?*

I always felt to be a part of music. Part of what it is in the world, and what it is to me on every level, including the soul, though I didn't always believe in the soul. For a while there I thought we were just examples of biology wandering the Earth with a small brain, trying to figure things out, and for what? To just die in the end?

Then I began to understand, by the mid- to late-Sixties, what had been quietly presenting itself to me my entire life long. Which is that we are all here for reasons much bigger than we can understand while living a human life. Life is much bigger—*we* are much bigger—than our understandings, our beliefs, our ideas, our obsessions. Those are small expressions of what we're doing or experiencing at the moment. They are not fully who we are.

For me, it didn't even come down to "This maharishi said this or that" or "This experimental drug experience showed me this." It was much bigger than that. Bigger than Timothy Leary or Allen Ginsberg or Dylan, or Yoko and me.

That was the mind-bending moment, when I saw that music is pure vibration. And that it's vibration with the potential to shift people's inner lives. Not only their minds, but their whole stance, their whole energy, and then everything they do and say and feel from there on.

It wasn't every musician who saw that, then or now. Many just respond to the music pouring out of them intuitively, which is great. If you just want to dance with it and see what happens, like you'd dance with a lover who knows you better than anyone else, who knows sides of you that you haven't even seen yet, then do that.

But after a time, I began to see that music was a doorway, and I had purposely sent myself through that portal to see what's on the other side of the human psyche. And what I mean by that, is that I needed to see what it is that's within us, that nearly every system on the planet does it damnedest to hide, squash, or destroy.

What is within us, that we are never supposed to know? Once I began asking those questions in bigger ways, I somewhat drew up my own death warrant.

**The old "power crowd" was using music to control young people to think, feel, be a particular way, and you were pointing to something much bigger than that. Something that connects us to the power of our own souls.**

Yes, though I wasn't the only one of course. Quite a few good people have left the Earth at their "behest," because those people were saying something the old elite have never wanted people to know.

Which is, for one, that they are only our "overlords" for as long as we let them be. That's the cornerstone, the key realization that many millions are tapping into now. That's a big part of why you see so many wars going on, journalists jailed and abused, even children jailed, abused, trafficked. They do this to dampen the human spirit into not only complacency, but the kind of numbness that comes with not being able to take any more bad news.

That makes you more pliable, because after a while you just sort of hunker down and hide, so that all the bad stuff won't find you.

And yet—look at what this group of young people in Florida[2] are doing now, taking on the gun lobby in the US! There are those taking on the legislators in the US and elsewhere who want to criminalize women for taking their own decisions about their own bodies. Others taking on the governments who deny climate change, or the armies who feel they have a right to commit genocide.

Those young people and others like them have a better understanding of the world than people three times their age, and they're saying No More. It's what we dreamt of in the Sixties and Seventies.

This time of awakening was inevitable in some ways, once the decision was made by the human race to awaken. It's just been met with extreme resistance by the au regime. More trauma that will need to be healed. Much of that healing is happening while people are on the Earth. Some will need to happen in other dimensions.

*But again—how do we overcome the fact that the invading races tampered with human DNA, and reduced the strands from 12 to only two? That took away our higher self insight.*

*I know that's changing now, but the average person doesn't know that, and certainly doesn't have control over it.*

You do have control over it! Every time you meditate, every time you connect with the Earth in a powerful and life-affirming

---

[2] John refers here to a group of survivors of the February 2018 mass shooting at Marjory Stoneman Douglas High School in Parkland, Florida. A group of students there quickly formed Never Again MSD, a political action committee working to increase gun control regulations.

way. Every time you listen to what you call high vibrational music, or heal yourself, or express yourself creatively or with pure higher intent—every time you dance or sing for the pure joy of it—all of those moments and others upgrade your DNA.

Those who have special connection to the element of air are lifted to a higher level as they stand in a storm or on a clifftop, with the wind roaring around them. Those with special connection to the water element experience it as they swim or stand under a waterfall. Those with special connection to the stars feel it as they look at the night sky. In those moments, you realize the Oneness of all Creation.

In addition to which, the Light coming into the planet now is highly transformative. You've never seen the like. I'd never have thought it possible while I was on the Earth plane. I thought you had to leave the body to move up into higher dimensional understanding and experience. Or meditate for months or years at a time. And maybe for most people then, that was the case. But no longer.

By the mid-Nineties, everything had shifted. The energy on the planet had moved up a grade. And by the end of 2012, it had done so again. Ascension full speed ahead, because that frequency moves higher every day now.

*But people have no idea what's happening to them!*

*Suppose I went around all day asking people, "How's your Ascension going? Feeling dizzy and exhausted, maybe depressed and fed up some days, elated and energized other days? No worries! You're just moving into the fifth dimension!"*

*Unless they were into that sort of thing, they'd think I was nuts.*

Well, you're only nuts in the sense that you've left the paradigm presented to you at birth. All "nuts" usually means is "sees things differently from the rest of us." Insanity has been too often defined as anyone who doesn't follow the rules. Those who break the rules in certain ways are called criminals, and those who take it to certain other levels are called mad as a hatter.

It's been that way for a long time. But it doesn't have to stay that way. Your generation was the first to really start changing things. People who were young during the Sixties or Seventies experienced the breakthroughs of that time, and are now taking part in early 21st century evolvement.

It's all one beautiful forward-moving arc. Yes, the "arc of justice" Dr King spoke of. And of overall progression.

*You look at it all so positively. From where I sit, it's just tiring and strange. I would like a bit more normalcy. I would like to feel more at home in the world. And I would like the madness—all the violence and upheaval—to finally cease.*

You are coming into that time. That is happening. It's just not able to pull ahead until you and millions, or even just thousands of others, decide you are only going to concentrate on Peace, abundance, equality, freedom. Within and without.

That day will come. You don't have to wait on anyone to create it for you. You're already creating it. Creating it from within.

*I choose to believe that's what's happening now.*

*I was watching the independent media news program Democracy Now! one evening when Yoko was on, and she was speaking very positively about free energy—geothermal and other methods.*

*The news anchor Amy Goodman said, "So you're very optimistic about all of this," and Yoko said that people will comment that to her sometimes, and she says to them, "I don't think we have any choice," which I thought was a great answer.*

*If we can't be optimistic and grounded in higher solutions, we lose the thread of progression.*

Yes! Exactly right.

*Going back to music for a moment, in this most recent Earth life in which so many knew your name, you were and still are known as a man who didn't take orders very well.*

*Not to say you couldn't collaborate with others. But as far as being the obedient employee, there was a block there. You understood early on that we weren't here to be robots.*

*How old were you when you realized that our whole system is set up for automatic responses and fear of "authority"?*

Very young—in a sense, almost right from the start. But more noticeably, maybe four or five years old. Definitely by the time I was at school. Not having a father around was a help there. Most British children grew up, post-World War II, hearing about how brave their fathers, grandfathers, uncles had been in one war or another. You were to respect them as if they were gods. You were never to question them.

If a woman was abused, it was considered to be her own fault or something she "asked for," and the man's right. If a child was abused, it was considered a shame, but something most people chose to overlook and not get involved in. This left plenty of room for testosterone to rule the day. So masculine authoritarian control had long ago overridden most matriarchal systems in British life.

I was fortunate in that I had strong women in my life—my mother, though her strengths were not always obvious to others, and my aunts and grandmother. And *still* I grew up a macho idiot! That didn't shift till the last few years of that life.

Our teachers generally toed the line the patriarchy had set. You've seen that quote, where my mother told me when I was small that the most important thing in life was to be happy. Then at school we were told to write down what we wanted to be when we grew up, and I said "happy"—an artist or a poet will make every verb a noun and every adjective an object.

And of course, the teacher saw my answer and said I hadn't understood the assignment. And I said, "You don't understand *life*," which got me called cheeky, and I caught a warning.

### But you were right!

Well, yes and no. Because for some people, the only way to be happy is not to just Be in the present moment. They have to be up and doing things they call fulfilling. Otherwise they feel their day is too empty for words. They fall into despair. They see themselves as a tool that needs a job to do. Most men view life that way.

This is why Yoko and I talked about staring at the clouds and understanding their messages. They already held meaning, just because they existed. It was up to us to discover it, not impose our beliefs on it. Just as it was up to us to imagine a better world. To have a powerful internal reality that could stand up to the tyranny of outer reality. And of course, so many just thought that was hilarious and bizarre.

Because for them, Doing overcame the art and practice of Being any day. But for some of us, it made perfect sense.

### Do you regret any of it—how you spent that Earth life?

Well, yes. I didn't treat women very well. And I wish I'd spent more time with my first son. A young man gets caught up in establishing himself in his work, and too often leaves the child-raising to the child's mother. And yet that was part of the au regime, the old system of patriarchy that without knowing it, I was learning how to stand up to.

And the hardest part to stand up to was my own unremitting use of that system. That I was the man and "what I say goes." I was still working on that when I left my body behind in 1980. But I'd come further by then than I'd ever thought possible.

After leaving Earth, the regret was not being able to be there for either son as they were growing up. All of that got muddled. It took a lot of adjustment. We don't measure time in Spirit as you do on Earth still, but I would say, it took a long time to accept that I had left the physical.

*I was in shock when I heard about it. Millions were, all over the world. I still say things like, "I wish he hadn't had to leave us when he did." Because your wisdom and understanding are badly needed now, as they were then.*

Do you think they'd have let me carry on being an activist millions of people listened to? It would have happened sooner or later. They'd have got rid of me eventually. I won't bore you with the details of exactly how and why it was arranged. But I somewhat felt it coming, and so did Yoko.

*Then why did you leave your apartment that day? She'd been consulting a psychic, and she begged you not to go out, didn't she?*

Because they weren't going to keep me captive in my own home! Because I'd have gone out at some point, and been their target another day, as much as that particular day.

Without knowing it, you and many other activists and Peace demonstrators have taken similar risks. It's just that you aren't as valuable a catch to them, because your circle of influence is not so large. In my case, things had happened politically that gave them cause to worry, or so they thought. So they acted, using an otherwise innocent, mentally ill man as their tool.

*They haven't won. "Give Peace A Chance" and #ImaginePeace are still powerful phrases heard round the world.*

*Yet from what I understand—switching back to music for a minute—you doubted that "Imagine" was a strong cut when it was first recorded. Meanwhile I hope most of us would have said, if we'd been there, "John, this song will change the world!"*

Perhaps in a way, many people's spirits were with me that day. And you all encouraged me energetically, as many have.

Outside of the crowds in music venues, I mainly only met people in that Earth life that I'd known in other lives. Most people have come to the Earth now on this timeline to finally settle matters with those they've known in other lives. This is a moment of reckoning on the Earth, on many levels. A finishing of old soul contracts, or a dissolving of them.

**So you'd known your wives and your sons in other lives, before this one? And your friends and fellow musicians as well?**

Of course I had. And yes, many of the people I performed and recorded with as well. I've been a musician or visual artist in a number of other lives. Sometimes fairly well known, sometimes somewhat known, and in other lives, utterly unknown.

Does fame really matter? No. If the music is going to go out and eventually reach round the world—if it's going to be transmitting higher frequencies and higher understanding to the world and all her people, does it matter whether the player is famous or not? No!

That's a misunderstanding people have—that you have to be famous to have any real impact on the world. Rubbish.

The reason it seems to be hugely significant, fame, is that when thousands of people are all singing the same song in an arena or even just watching something on television, film, the internet, they're all of one mind in that moment.

And say the particular chord they've struck in that moment is one of, "Why are we at war with one another? Why is anyone left hungry? How is it that anyone could be homeless, have no medical care, or no education? How can we allow injustices to occur to our Earth or our fellow human?"—*that* is a powerful moment! You can't calculate the power of it.

Because that is when you collectively decide *We're going to change things*, and that threatens the old powers-that-were as some call them. Nowhere near so powerful as they seem, but then mental conditioning and spiritual downgrading was always their game, so they could hide behind the illusion. They have lost that game now, of course.

But those moments can be created through the inner connection of thousands or millions of people, holding the same vision at once. They don't have to be physically together in one place.

### When did it start to occur to you that music could change the world?

When you're entertaining thousands of screaming adolescents at a large venue, it's hard to miss. They wouldn't just jump up and down. They would faint, some of them, or wet their pants. They would look as if they were losing their minds. "Will they find them again?" is something we would wonder.

And we hoped in a way they wouldn't find their minds again, if it meant they would be ruled by dry, dull studies that were outside their interests, then fall into dry, dull jobs that would beat their spirits down into the ground over time.

That was wishful thinking on our part, but it was our hope— and maybe for some, we were a help that way.

### A psychologist would say it was all hormones— teenage madness.

And yet it wasn't. It was much bigger than that. We were a sort of doorway. A demonstration of doing things your own way and finding your own life.

None of us were raised to be professional musicians. Far from it. We fought for it. We challenged the norm. It helped that we had nothing to lose, and doubted at first that it would last—the band, or rock music. We disciplined ourselves, as you know, playing the clubs in Hamburg, honing our craft in eight-hour shifts. We weren't going to get any worse, playing for long stretches like that. And then once we started performing our own work, and stopped trying to be Elvis or whoever, it all grew up from there.

*People are still pretty nostalgic about the four of you—magazines proclaimed in early 2019, "55 years since the Beatles arrived at JFK Airport!" As if we could bring back the innocence of those times.*

*Yet those days weren't all that innocent. We were already in Viet Nam. We'd just lost a president. It's just that we choose to remember our youth in happier terms. I was still tiny in 1964, but I loved the four of you almost as much as the teenagers did. It was like we had been waiting for you.*

*I cherished my sister's Beatles lunchbox. I'd sing Beatle songs at the top of my lungs, on the swings at preschool. Making my teacher none too happy, because the neighbors complained about the noise.*

Everybody's a critic!

*That's the truth, friend!*

*So you're saying that in a way, because of what your life mission was, music chose you.*

Several art forms chose me. Music was just the clearest outlet for what I came to say. And I am grateful to it for all it gives us. It was my saving grace many days—the only way I could keep my sanity and see who I was, and why I was alive at that time. The thing I had to do.

Everyone has one of those things.

If you have that kind of impetus pushing you along, you doubt the quality of your work less often, because it's less a matter of "Is this song any good?" and more a matter of "This is something that needs to be said."

That kind of realization changes everything.

# 6

# The Power to Re-Create

*I hardly recognize my own country anymore.*
*Middle class life is all but gone in the United States.*
*Half the households in the country go without some*
*basic every month, like adequate food or medical*
*care, or paying the electric bill. Homelessness is*
*on the rise, especially now that millions have been*
*further impoverished during the pandemic. College*
*loan debts are out of control.*

*If you were on the Earth right now, mired in debt*
*with barely a middle income or a lower income, and*
*just lost your health insurance or some other vital*
*service, what would you do to keep yourself from*
*falling into ongoing anger or despair?*

*How would you use your ingenuity to pull*
*yourself out of this ridiculous system? To rise above*
*it somehow?*

Nearly anyone can rise above it. I'm no guru there. The
most vital thing, and the hardest thing, is to avoid the ongoing

anger and despair you speak of. That's what pulls you under the rising waters—not the amount of money owed, or the basic necessities that have to be done without half the time. People can survive a lot. But despair is a killer beyond most.

There's no great breakthroughs of thought and invention—the kind you need to get yourself out of a tough situation—till you come out of emotional upset. Though sometimes a complete low point morphs into a moment of awakening. So then you refuse to stay on the track you're on, and deliberately set out to create a far higher one.

When you're ready—when you declare and announce to your guides that you're ready for Solutions and nothing less, the right idea will arrive.

Usually, you have to call out for higher forms of help to come to you. They can't intervene otherwise, unless your guardians see you're about to fall off your path. The one you carved out for yourself before being born on Earth again. They're always right there with you, ready to help. If you ask for their input every day, you don't need to wait till things go upside down before you make a shift.

Every human being carries a certain amount of weight on their back as they move through life. The question is, *how* is it carried? It's not about the situation. It's about how you view it. How you feel about it. What you conclude about it. And whether you feel the Universe is on your side or not.

## You can very consciously awaken to what you have unconsciously helped to create, without self-blame.

So the first step isn't changing things outwardly. It's realizing, *I'm not owned by this situation—not by debt, or high cost of living, or competition for a home or a job, or being turned down for a loan or a raise. This does not define me. I'm far bigger than that. I revel in my strength, and my independence from outer situations. I deal with those situations, but I don't source my outlook from them. I keep the Light burning within, always.*

That's how a prisoner keeps their energy calm and positive, even when surrounded by cement blocks and barbed wire. That's how the war refugee manages to get by on the slightest scraps of food, without losing hope. And that's how the mother raising her children on her own manages to keep her perspective fresh, and her energy strong. They have their moments of shock and dismay. But those who stay positive know their outer situation no more owns them than the egg owns the hen.

The next step, I would say—not a happy one—is realizing that you've been a part of the situation you're in, whether you realize it or not. Part of this is your own unspoken, deeply held expectation or unconscious pattern.

Most likely, these are buried in your DNA from your culture and ancestors, and all the subconscious conditioning you've been prey to all your life. They're almost always a powerful part of what you're experiencing. Past lives also weigh in as a powerful influence.

And the majority of people write setbacks and challenges into their life plan, before incarnating, to finally iron out some old issue, or to learn from it.

None of it's an accident, though it will feel that way some days. No need to blame yourself. But there is a great need to move on from despair, or just feeling like you always come up empty. Don't ever let it become a habit.

The next step, and it's a happier one, is realizing you can *very consciously awaken to what you have unconsciously helped to create*, without self-blame. (Yes, even humanity's decision to live in duality for eons.) From there, you can start to realize that you are absolutely able to create something much better than that.

## Goldmines of ingenuity and creativity remain powerfully within you, and are rising to the surface.

Most people despise hearing that they had anything to do with how things have worked out for them. They want to believe that nothing of what they're suffering now is connected to their energies or ideas, or influences they can't even see. They want to believe that it just happened. That life just happens to people. But I'm not talking about it being someone's "fault." No one is blaming them or anyone.

I'm saying, start looking at your situation as something you have the power to not only create but to *re-create*. To remedy and revise. Start looking at it as something you can mold with your own thought, feeling, intent. The right ideas applied at the right time. Expectations and images of what you want, instead of running on and on about what you don't want. Because in that moment that you complain and feel defeated, you're only creating more of the same.

You've all heard it many times: *All the Universe can do is create what you express as being true—what you project and feel to be true in the present moment.*

So yes, you're seeing injustice happening on a broad scale. You're lucky if you're only out of money, and not one of the several million in prison in the US, for having done little to nothing, most of them. Born black, red, or brown, mainly— that's their only "crime." Or caught with marijuana one too many times.

And yes, it is a kind of prison sentence to be in debt, and to stress daily over making ends meet. Or to be ill, or see a loved one ill. I wouldn't say otherwise. It's just that if you are in that situation, you're both the prisoner and the guard.

The minute your emotions and descriptions of that situation begin to metamorphosize into something more positive—the more you accept the situation and bless it, as some would say, instead of cursing it, find a reason to give thanks for whatever you do have—that's the minute things start to change. You begin to step into mastery. Mastering your circumstances instead of feeling crushed by them. And your situation finds room to move to a much higher level.

Yes, it hears you and responds.

At that point, you're no longer trapped and troubled by your circumstances. You wake up. You realize you're being put through your paces, in terms of co-Creating a better life. You're calling out to the Spirit of Transformation.

You can transform a situation, just by saying to it, "Thank you, friend. I see you're crying out for my Love and attention. So I'm going to start taking better care of you. Thank you for allowing me to create a situation that shows me how you're doing. Which is not great, going by outer appearances. So I'm going to spend more time appreciating you and sending you Love, not criticism."

That could be about anything—your physical shape or health, your finances, your home, your relationship. You're telling it, "I'm going to start seeing all the things going right with you, and praising them to the skies. And if I get the urge to complain, I'll stop myself, and say, *I'm glad for what I have. And everything good here is increasing, many times over.*"

You really have to kind of proclaim it. Because the kind of carefully constructed degradation of the working person that you describe is obviously not accidental. And it's only partly about money and power and control. It's mainly about distracting you from what's really happening in the world, and even more than that, putting you into such a state of helplessness, despair, and passivity, that that becomes your overriding vibration.

Let me tell you, I have seen the human race and what it has become—what it is still becoming—over these past 40 years of Earth time, and it not helpless or weak. It may be at times resentful or feel to be at a loss. But goldmines of ingenuity and creativity remain powerfully within you, and are rising to the surface.

You've all got deeply buried memories of the ancient and pre-ancient mystery schools, and their manifestation teachings, their metaphysical teachings that explain the Universal laws. You still remember on some level who you were and what roles you played in the great societies of Lemuria, Atlantis, Sumeria, and similarly advanced cultures on your home planets.

You've all come here to remember and reclaim all that, at the most demanding of times. I say this knowing that the human race has suffered tremendously over thousands of years of enslavement and unconsciousness, during which time humans were told that the gods were displeased with them. That they were being punished with cruel weather and illness and injury and hunger and death. You have now surpassed those ancestors on nearly every level.

So surpass them on this level as well! Don't stop now, with this great rolling out of empowerment and the beauty of who you really are! Refuse to be outdone, because you are not outnumbered. Release the need to allow your mind to tell you what is OK and what isn't. When to panic and when to finally feel all right about things.

The mind is very small still. It's been systematically downsized in capability over millennia, and responds to certain stimuli with panic, sadness, and feelings of defeat, regardless of what your soul or higher self sees.

You will have days when you wonder why you came, how you can possibly go on, and what you could possibly do differently to come up with a different result.

And I will tell you, friends: You are doing incredibly well. You are brave and powerful, just by virtue of the fact that you are a human being on this planet in these strange yet transformative times.

No one can encapsulate, imprison, or restrain you now, energetically speaking, unless you let them. In these energies, you will only continue to regain your equilibrium and independence. Continue to gain strength and to create inventive designs and solutions, so that everybody wins. You're well releasing the idea that the old way of doing things is the only way. You'll continue to know your own power to transform a situation by how you view it. By what you call it, and what you expect of it.

Your emotions come first in this, even before your thoughts. You've been taught the opposite. The patriarchal system demands that people value the mind over the heart, every time. Deny them that. They don't deserve your "obedience." And you have no more to give there. It's played out, that scheme.

*I follow what you're saying, but don't you feel that it's a way of turning your back on your fellow suffering human—the impoverished elderly, the veterans, the homeless, the immigrants held in the camps, to say, "I'm going to think positively from now on. I'm only going to see and give thanks for the good in everything."*

*Doesn't that sort of deny what people are going through? If just a few of us save ourselves while others are still suffering—is that a solution? I get lost on that point, even though I really prefer to think and feel positively about everything.*

*I agree with the theory. I've seen things transform in my and other people's lives, once our ideas and emotions about a situation transformed. It's just bizarre at times, because it's the opposite of what we're taught.*

*And hearing you say all this, people might wonder, When did he stop being a 'Working Class Hero?' "*

They can think whatever they like. It's of no consequence to me, what people think, and it should be of no consequence to you, whether they think you or I have abandoned them by refusing to join them in living purely in reaction to life.

What I'm encouraging is what I spoke of before, and what I had started doing while I was still on the Earth plane—to seek inner action, followed by inspired outer action.

And it's increasingly occurring to millions of people that the inner revolution is the one that's needed now. If all they want is for us to despair and give up, and forget how powerful the new human is now, I should think you'd be the first one to say, "Forget it—I'm not going down that road."

And then dedicate yourself to rising above appearances. That's how they've fooled humanity for millennia—with appearances. And the idea that the one who rises above the pack has abandoned the folk they came from. When in fact, all that does is inspire others to do the same. It's a huge gift to them.

*I would think so too, but I only get there part of the time.*

All right then—praise that part! Be glad for it! Celebrate it. Because if you don't notice the hurdle you've cleared, every time you decide to reign above your circumstances, instead of being owned and run over by them—you're missing the party! One of the biggest ever thrown.

There's your sovereignty, right there. That's the planet's sovereignty. One person after another, claiming their independence from what appears to be real.

*People get angry when you encourage them to stop feeling bad about life. They want you to join them in being unhappy, in reacting. I can certainly show compassion, but what they want is for someone to resonate on their level, which brings my energy down. They want a companion for where they are in that moment.*

Of course. But that's their lower self. It's the ego-mind as people call it. It's the shadow self, and not *them*, exactly. They are actually beautifully in charge, powerful, and positive at all times. They just don't know their true selves. Run by cultural programming, DNA codes, the presence of ancestors, interfering energies—all of that gets very confusing. It covers the true self.

Add to that the trauma felt not only in this life but in many others, and the push to accomplish their soul contracts, their Earth mission. The desire to rise above Earth conditions.

Often, people's spirits release from their bodies in their sleep state at night (though still connected to them) so that their consciousness can return to their home planet, or command their own starships, or meet with their twin flame and soul family. Or whatever brings them joy—swimming with the whales and dolphins, soaring over the mountains and rivers.

You and many others have had dreams where you were flying, or in a spacecraft, or in a council meeting with those involved in a common mission. Most of that is actual experience. In those moments, human beings rejoin who they really are. Not as fully as when they soul-merge, but pretty powerfully, I would say.

*But we don't live there consciously all the time. We live here on Earth where things have gone mad, at least for the moment. Where we are still working people, grappling with the day to day.*

You know, I only ever used the term "working class hero" kind of sardonically. And I wouldn't use it now, because I've released the class or economic caste system, and so must you. Release it and all its symbols. It's nothing but a trap. The more you release the need to prove yourself financially, to achieve this or that, the freer you will be. And I know you are not in the category of those thinking they need a bigger house or a fancier vehicle to be happy. Most people aren't.

But you help yourself more when you say, "I always have more than enough abundance." More than enough money, good health, love, support, solutions. And the inner means to create what you need.

Most people are blocked energetically by many things in every Earth life. In this particular Earth life you are all in, you've come in to release yourselves from those blocks, and to allow in more power, more Light, more brilliance, into every cell.

That's not something someone can do *for* you, though energy workers gain in ability every day. It's something you've got to hold in your energies as a powerful intent—that you will not be held back. That you will not be imprisoned by the effects of low energies.

## Your subconscious will react powerfully and positively to the right symbols and images, so use them!

It's true that Earth and all her beings are moving into the fifth dimension now. And so the world is experiencing what feels like a tornado raging through, or an earthquake where all the old structures fall onto the ground in a heap. That is not always smooth or pleasant. It's what has to happen some days, for the new to have room to come in. That's how it works in terms of Universal Law, and that's how it works in your own lives as well.

Release the habit of speaking negatively about any part of life. Watch your words. You have no idea how powerful, how co-creative they are. Stop yourself from saying you're broke, because you're not. Stop saying your health or your job or your country is lost or in trouble. Release the old vibration. The old paradigm. It was set up to defeat you.

Keep in mind, as well, that some of the unsureness people are experiencing is the feeling that all of humankind is starting something completely new. The old ego-mind construct will read that as a potential danger, but it isn't. It's the excitement of a new era beginning. So be aware that those inner signals can get crossed. Because you've still got the old survival instincts at work in your conscious and subconscious. But you can get past that.

I would say to anyone now, get a few books on abundance and manifestation methods, and use them! Put up symbols in your home for whatever you want to create, for your higher good to come in. Place gold or gold-colored objects in the wealth sector of your home, if you know your feng shui. And open your arms wide each day, and saying, "Health, wealth, happiness—all forms of abundance, flow to me now! Thank you for being here, always!"

The Universe loves that sort of thing. Don't ask me why—it's just a symbol-driven place. Not only word-driven, though words are potent. They release intent out into the air, and from there, the energy begins to gather to make it happen. Most people are not yet fully aware of how certain words are imbued with very low, imprisoning energies, while others are full of freedom and fulfillment.

Take my word for it. People plus words, and people plus symbols, are powerful combinations.

But be Light about it. Laugh and have fun with it. Be a child with a toy. Don't hang the weight of your hopes and dreams on any one practice, or you drain it of its vitality.

Respect the power of your words, then go beyond them! Hold beautiful images in your mind as you meditate, and put up positive images in your home whenever you can. Give your subconscious a chance to leap over all the gates and roadblocks it carries. It will react powerfully and positively to the right symbols and images, so use them!

There's no need to despair. That's just another lie.

And you're not fooled by those anymore.

# 7

# Starships and Sacred Missions

*You've mentioned ETs and starships. You actually witnessed a ship one evening in August 1974. It was on a weekend, and your part of Manhattan was nearly empty, as so many people were away. When you phoned the police to report the sighting, they said other people had called in about it as well.*

*You tell the story of standing on the balcony of your apartment and seeing this huge, silver metal, round ship full of lights hovering about 100 feet away from you. And you took photos of it.*

*What else happened during that experience that you haven't shared before? And why do you think the prints of the photos were blank, when you got them back from the developer?*

You're right that there's a bit more to the story than what I told in interviews.

I had been asking for proof that we weren't the only ones— that humans weren't the only race on the planet and in the

Universe. I was asking people who seemed to know about that. And asking whoever might be able to hear my thoughts and intentions, that they show themselves and make it clear that we are from the stars, that we're all connected.

After saying that all people on Earth are interconnected, the next step would have been to realize that all life in the Universe is interconnected. That we're not alone. That we have a lot to learn from those who live on a higher vibrational level than humanity does.

People who were well-versed in that subject were sharing experiences and information with me, and I could tell from the way they spoke that while some were quite idealistic, none of them were mad. They weren't making it up or hallucinating. It was too chancy in those days for most people to go public in a big way with their or others' experiences of nonterrestrials, or ship sightings, though several did just that.

Sometimes they were ridiculed, but often their ideas and experiences were accepted as an "alternative viewpoint" or "possibly true but not scientifically proven." Most people had no time for the idea that we're not the only ones here. It didn't seem real or important to them. Or they would just laugh at it. That's what people have been trained to believe—that it was nonsense or fiction.

When the first *Star Wars* film came out, I realized that things were shifting in a very big way. Because now a whole generation of young people were seeing images and experiences on the big screen that they related to powerfully. Intuitively, they knew it was real, what they were seeing. They knew they'd seen it somewhere—in their dreams, or in other lives, or maybe even in this life in some way.

It wasn't just someone's imagination.

And as you know, *Star Wars* came from a real story that Lucas received from a spirit who spoke through a channeler and revealed actual people and histories. He didn't just make it up, any more than *Star Trek* was completely made up. And the timing of that show and the *Star Wars* films was perfect. They presaged the Light that's pouring into the planet now, which is opening up people's energies and reviving buried memories, and reminding them of who they really are.

## Most people on Earth have at least one ship watching over them at all times.

Once I began to realize the enormity of that—as much as I could at the time—I felt almost overwhelmed by the possibilities of it all. I realized that there were beings who had the solutions to everything wrong with our Earth, and all the ways she was suffering. That they had cures for every illness, and new forms of thought and capability. That they probably used all or nearly all their brain power, while we humans used only a tiny percentage of ours.

And that they lived without currency, without poverty, without religions, without wars and other separations between peoples. Never mind the higher technology. The consciousness was the astounding part.

*My question is, do you think you were downloaded with information by whoever was in that ship? Maybe they revealed to you some aspect of your life mission that hadn't occurred to you yet.*

*Maybe they'd been nearby your whole life, and just decided to reveal themselves to you at that point—?*

We're all in touch with beings from other planets and solar systems all the time. Some of these people are in our soul group, and are working alongside us in our soul mission for that particular lifetime. Others are just curious, or maybe from our home planet. There's a wide spectrum of possibilities there.

I wouldn't call it so much a download, as an interactive transmission. Because it's not just you or me receiving. It's a conversation. We open up to receive this Light data to not only evolve ourselves, but the planet as a whole. Then we start to relate to ourselves and the Earth in a higher way. And not all contact moments are well-intended. But I would say that the majority of them are, particularly now.

Most people on Earth have at least one ship watching over them at all times—their crew, that is, unless the ship is completely sentient in and of itself, and functions as a sort of guardian. The only exception would be people who have stated on some level of consciousness that they want nothing to do with those of a higher dimensional frequency, who live at a much higher level of consciousness. And higher dimensional beings working in the Light do respect that decision.

But even those who have chosen that are now noticing things they would never have noticed even a few years ago, in terms of their own thought processes. They're feeling an increasing curiosity to know what else is here, or "out there." The way they view the planet in general is shifting—they're more seeing her as a living being than a big lump of clay.

It is absolutely true that ships will reveal themselves to people sometimes, but not at other times, and to some people but not others, even if the others are standing right next to them. When that ship appeared to me and May[3] that day in New York, I couldn't believe there wasn't a crowd gathered on the street below. But so few people look *up* as they're walking in New York. And when I thought about it later, I realized maybe we were meant to see it, and most others weren't, for various reasons. Though yes, some did see it.

People forget too, that there are higher dimensional beings walking the Earth who appear to be just your average human, though they're well beyond that. There are many beings whose vibrational and molecular density is not so thick and heavy as the average person's. So that just as with the higher vibrational ships, those beings aren't fully visible to the eye for the most part.

Children and babies, animals, a scarce few adults with special sight—they can see them. Babies will even point to them, just as they point to Angels floating high in the corner of the room.

But not most adults, no. Because by the age of seven or so, the left brain has been trained to dominate the right brain. The rational mind declares itself superior in all ways, and denies that anything is real other than what it's taught or what it has already experienced.

---

[3] John is referring here to May Pang, who was his partner for a while in the mid-Seventies, during a split from his wife Yoko Ono.

And of course, that's what the powers-that-were call "education"—telling people what not to believe, over and against their own intuitive knowing, which is there even when they're still in the womb. It's powerfully connected to human spirit. It's the voice of the spirit or the higher self, the intuition is.

So to silence that voice, the left-brain aspect of thought and understanding has been overemphasized in nearly every area of life, in nearly every culture. What they meant in the old days by "civilizing" any Native indigenous people was driving out their intuitive ability, and their sense of their own Divinity, and replacing it with what the colonizers called Religion and Science.

And in that indoctrination, the Masculine has been touted as superior to and stronger than the Feminine on all levels. So that form of white male domination is well covered by that system as well.

*Yet now the spirit of the Divine Feminine has returned to the Earth plane. Divine Mother is here! Mother Sekhmet is here. Quan Yin is here. Mary Magdalene is here. Mary, Mother of Jesus. Lady Master Portia. Lady Master Nada. Lady Master Lilith. And thousands of other representations of the Divine Feminine. You can see that coming out now in every corner of life.*

Another reason why it's safer now to talk about having witnessed a craft, or a Sasquatch being, or to talk about spiritual awakening. Or to speak of having met someone who spoke and looked rather odd compared to most people, with the intuitive realization that that's because they're impersonating an Earth human, but weren't actually born one.

While on Earth, I spoke with people who had met some of those people, and it makes you wonder . . .

*Well, those who have been running the planet for millennia aren't from here, as you say. And from what I understand, they do impersonate us. They and certain other races can and do shapeshift at will. The Navajo still speak of Skinwalkers—people who change their outer shape and appearance to suit a situation.*

*The Native peoples have always been powerfully in touch with the Star Nations. They trace their beginnings from them. The more benevolent star beings taught them how to plant and grow crops millennia ago. That's part of Native history and oral tradition. Many people around the world know about it, except those who need to hear it most.*

Yet they are hearing it. Even their resistance to new ideas is a good sign. That annoyed or incredulous look means their minds are opening up and at least entertaining a new idea long enough to consider it worthy of discussion. At least now the idea exists. It's in the arena.

And once it's in the arena of thought and experience, once enough people admit, "This is something we talk about, even if only to laugh about it," then it becomes increasingly real to them.

Then people start saying, "Maybe we've missed something here. Maybe we should take a deeper look at this." Look at the success of the series *The X Files*! That's proof that people are utterly hungry for information so long denied them. So long ridiculed as unthinkable.

And so—if it's so impossible, why are we talking about it?

*You feel it's the next step in the planet's evolution, to realize that we're becoming part of an intergalactic society? And that to avoid that reality is to deny a big part of our identity?*

Yes. Because it is true that there are powerful governmental, military, and corporate structures in place to ensure that people don't hear about or spend much time thinking about the possibility of an undisclosed space program. One that well outsizes what you know of NASA.

Yet the rising consciousness of humanity is now beginning to outweigh the effects of those disguises. And they've been in place for centuries. Generally people don't know about all of these secret operations until they're briefed on them, once they've stepped into a role in one of those corporate hives.

**There are billions of nonterrestrial beings
watching the Earth and assisting her in
transitioning to a higher dimension
as smoothly as possible.**

Things have changed since 1974, in a big way. The photos I took of that ship didn't come out because the ETs contacting me and others had to protect us. Now you see photos of ships all over the internet. Some have been ships that were reverse-engineered by your military (based on ET ships), and some are genuinely from other planets or stars. But it's become a part of everyday life, whereas it wasn't at that time.

The vast majority of ET spotters and believers are left alone by the old powers-that-were. There are too many of you to bother with. Mass mind control is used instead of individual surveillance and harassment, because it's simplest and covers so much of Earth's population.

The slight problem now with their plan, is that people are becoming increasingly cognizant of the mind control, and once the wizard behind the curtain is spotted, that tends to mean the beginning of the end of that and the more subtle forms of control.

***And those are technologies that almost no one can hear or see, but which everyone is subject to.***

Yes, except that people who hold a very high vibrational frequency—and most only get there with real focus and clear intent—are able to float above even the technological forms of manipulation. This is why you see quite a number of enlightened spiritual teachers on the Earth now, of varying ages and backgrounds. And then there are those you don't see—the children who are coming in with such a high vibration that they are utterly immune to those transmissions.

This explains the push to mandate certain shots for children, with substances that lower their DNA frequency and content—their DNA "reach" you might say, which are like antennae for the Light data. The old regime is aware that those coming in aren't affected by the only technologies they've used to manipulate and control. That's scaring the daylights out of them.

Note that higher vibrational music is now being heard more and more. The music that holds not only a higher hertz resonance, but which reflects or carries the music of the spheres. That can awaken nearly anyone over time, and they don't even have to concentrate. They just have to welcome in those frequencies by welcoming in the music.

**And you're working with people who are still on the Earth to help them bring in more of that higher vibrational music?**

Yes, I am, and it's a glorious adventure! And I'm probably able to do more here in the spiritual realm than I would be able to do if I were an old man on the Earth. We've been at it a while. I meet with the souls of those willing to be born into Earth lives where they will birth this music in their Earth life. Then I am in touch with them as guide and mentor as they begin to actually do that. Some of them while still quite young.

You're witnessing all forms of genius from those who have been born in these last 30 years or so. They are astounding. They well outshine the generations before them. But then, everyone comes in with a particular Earth mission at a particular point on Earth's current timeline, for reasons that are beyond anyone. And that must be respected.

Many are in awe of these young people. Not only for their technical genius, but for their prescience, their prophetic outlook. They see where the world is headed, and what will happen if Earth issues aren't handled wisely and powerfully now. They see it all.

**Some days I feel there is very little hope for Earth's current systems, and then I remember that these are fading so that new and higher vibrational forms can be birthed.**

**I'm just wondering in what soil those new forms are being planted, because the troubles I see on the planet now—you've named a number of them—are so deep-seated and severe, they feel to be unsolvable.**

57

They are not solvable under the current paradigm the planet is run on, no. There are numerous bad seeds to be removed before Earth will know the kind of Peace that you envision for her and her inhabitants—animals and humans, soil and air, water and plants and minerals. All of it contaminated and misdirected for millennia.

So what is occurring instead is that the old is being supplanted by the new. This is why you're hearing about ideas such as universal income and free healthcare. Packaging that breaks down in a bio-friendly way. Hemp being used instead of plastic. Free energy. Sustainable housing. These are not even the major shifts that are fully needed, but they are steps in the right direction that fifty years ago, would have been a pipe dream.

**So higher vibrational living is being interwoven with our current Earth life, to assist in the much bigger transition?**

Yes it is! I want to say, "You have no idea," but then you'll ask for particulars, and I can't give those right now. And much of it is still being written. But if you feel things are becoming more egalitarian, more open-minded, and geared to assisting people in accepting the provisions of NESARA law[4], that would be correct.

**One of my biggest questions is, do you think we will survive climate change, as a human race? Will the Earth survive?**

The Earth is always going through changes. There is no way to avoid that. She has seen powerful changes in her climate in the past, and in her terrain and chemical makeup, and she will

---

[4] John refers here to the National Economic Security and Reformation Act (NESARA), signed into law by President Clinton in October 2000, but not yet enacted, as of this writing. Beginning in the United States before extending to all nations throughout the world, NESARA will end war, end income taxes, and end the Federal Reserve, among other reforms. It will also oversee the release of free energy devices and thousands of long-suppressed healing technologies, among many other provisions.

continue to see these transitions. It's not a huge surprise, if you consider all the different eons-long ages that have occurred on the planet over millions of years.

You stand at the cusp of the new Earth era, and that can feel both intimidating and thrilling some days. Panic will not help you—not in this issue or any other, whether you're concerned for your own life or that of billions of people. So all need to remain calm and centered as they say, and ask for higher wisdom on this issue, because it's a big one.

And yes, I do see Earth surviving these shifts.

## You have countless intergalactic cultures keeping a watch on Earth as the living being she is, and countless higher beings assisting in the etheric.

You may feel you are not going down this road on your own, and that would be correct. There are billions of nonterrestrial beings watching the Earth and assisting her in transitioning to a higher dimension as smoothly as possible—as much as they can, without breaking Universal Law. They can't do a complete overhaul of the current situation, and you would feel intruded upon and interfered with if they did. But they do what they can to help mitigate the more devastating and extreme effects of the climate shifts.

You've been witnessing earthquakes, volcanic eruptions, sudden fires, floods, and shifts in precipitation and temperature that seem just outrageous. Some of that is climate change. Some of it is due to weather manipulation by higher technologies, to affect certain populations or to try (unsuccessfully) to dampen the Light being anchored in certain parts of the planet, as she gains in resonance and an overall higher vibration.

Earth's vibration affects the population's vibration, which is basically the whole of human consciousness. It would be impossible now to diminish the metamorphosis of that Light-enhanced awakening. Yet weather manipulation seeks to do that, as well as to ruin the economies and autonomy of whole populations.

This is why you see extreme drought in some continents, as former water sources have now dried up. And why you see extreme rain or snow followed by flooding in other regions, and fires in others. If the dark side could make 95 percent of the planet unlivable, they would do so.

Yet they will not be allowed to destroy the planet, through any means.

Again—this is not something to be despondent about. You are not alone in facing these situations. You have countless intergalactic cultures keeping a watch on Earth as the living being she is, and countless higher beings assisting in the etheric. Both are actively in touch with Earth's inhabitants and working with them as scientists, visionaries, healers, and alchemists to assist in the stabilization of the planet. You have your soul families, and your own higher selves involved in this.

Yes, some of the human race are choosing to leave at this time. You have noticed this. But often that is a choice made based on their higher self's desire to assist while in the etheric, rather than in the physical.

I and many others in the higher realms, who understand the despair felt by many now, are working with Light Beings who are sending healing Light and messages of encouragement to those dealing with overwhelm, depression, and anger. The presence of all who have come with a path of Light is very much needed on the Earth now.

You are every one of you here for a sacred, powerful, beautiful reason that will become clearer and clearer to you, the longer you journey this path.

You all chose this path for very big reasons, and the fog has already started to lift.

# 8

# Our Daughters' Voices

*May we talk about your relationships with women in this last Earth life? Because you got fairly honest and self-critical after a while, about how you had treated women when you were younger, and your relationships with your wives.*

*So it looked like you caught on after a while that you'd been, as you called yourself at one point, a "macho working class Northern man." And that that meant having a lot of preconceived ideas and expectations that aren't necessarily positive for a relationship.*

You're right when you say it's not positive! Women have been treated like second class citizens, denied a vote on family and community decisions, even over their own lives, for so long. And of course what you've seen over the past 50-some years is that they are demanding to have control over their lives, and equal say in all areas of life. And thankfully, the idea that women should put up with the old system has faded in many parts of the world.

Unfortunately, there are still real income disparities in the so-called developed world, and in many countries, great disparities between male and female in terms of education, health rights, and personal, social, and political rights.

You're aware that for so long, there was this pressure laid on from social and religious teachings, that women were to revere and allow a man's decisions about most things. Men were supposedly more rational, more adult, more reliable. Closer to God, and absolved of wrong since it was Eve who handed Adam the apple, as the story goes. A story whose true origins have been entirely obscured and lied about.

So that billions over the centuries were told to uphold the man's beliefs and preferences as being the only real ones to live by. Because, well—look! Jesus was a man. Buddha was a man. Abraham and Mohammed were male. And God is clearly male, because he's always referred to as male in the sacred texts (translated and edited entirely by men, all references to Divine Feminine removed). So that means men are different—better and special compared to women and children.

Clearly, it means they're meant to hold dominion over other beings who are smaller and shaped differently, because men are also naturally stronger, and wiser! And can therefore give hell to anyone questioning them, if that's the mood they're in.

Most modern women can immediately see the madness in that, because they see through the false reasoning behind what are basically male supremacy teachings, which easily and naturally became white male supremacy teachings. And that in turn supports certain Euro-centric institutions in raping and pillaging whole cultures and whole continents. And they have done.

Because if men are superior to women and children, then clearly, *some* men are superior to other men. And of those— those of a certain race, religion, social standing—there's a smaller minority who are even more superior to the others. And an even smaller, more exclusive subset drawn from that crowd. And *those* men in turn answer to an even smaller minority, who rule over all.

Lovely system! It worked (miserably) for thousands of years. Till now.

**So tell me what you see happening now on that front, from where you sit.**

What I see now is a miracle, compared to those eons of oppression. What I see now, is the average person standing up in a way they never knew they could before. The difference being that they're not waiting for anyone's permission to stand up.

They're just saying, "Our lives matter," whether they're refugees or nonwhites or women or teens or even animals, because the animals also speak. They just do it telepathically and biochemically.

What you have with any form of presumed supremacy is a hierarchy, and a hierarchy always depends on duality—the good/bad, light/darkness, male/female, Left/Right construct. Branches of opposites that play off one another, that war on and off for centuries. All of it based on what are supposedly sacred texts, that have been crafted so as to set people against not only one another, but also the Earth, and even whole aspects of their own spirit and psyche.

That's the idea—to divide the inner self into parts, each of them disparaging and disapproving of all the other parts. With a war raging within you, you have little time to feel integrated and empowered enough to stand up to the divisions you see out in the world, because you're even at odds with yourself. Huge portions of your life energy are then lost in that great gaping hole that comes from lacking Love and acceptance of yourself.

The more your own separate aspects dislike and criticize one another ("Why are you eating/watching/saying that?" "Shut up! Because I want to!"), the more you'll criticize and disapprove of those around you.

And of course, the great enabler of that horrible system is the ego-mind itself. The rational, overly analytical, "Let's talk this to death" left-brain aspect of the human mind that was trained to squash the capabilities of the right-brain. Yet that right-brain aspect is your saving grace many days. It thinks in metaphors and symbols. It outruns the training you received as a child that said you weren't good enough to stand before God or people.

### What I wish I'd done differently, and will do differently in a new life, is to realize that every human being is an expression of Divinity.

It offers you solutions, and reminds you of how endless your inner vision can be. It can reveal new explorations and inventions that would cure whole areas of deprivation and suffering on the planet. But that visionary aspect has to be trusted and used at least 10 or 20 percent of the time.

You've heard spiritual teachers go on about the beauty of the heart-mind—how it lives in the Present Moment, and envisions higher forms of living. How it can forgive and accept both the self and others in ways the ego-mind never could.

The heart-mind has room to come in when the left and right brain are balanced and integrated. Though humanity was once downgraded to two-strand DNA, and the left and right hemispheres were separated, you are evolving beyond that now. I am basically saying that the duality, the male/female aspects of the psyche facing off against one another, one demanding slavery from the other (and both male and female have had their time at that), has ended.

It may not look that way, as you look at certain cultures. But those energy waves from the Great Central Sun are coming in and powerfully affecting everyone on Earth, whether they are aware of that or not. They are impossible to stop at this point.

My feeling is, even the interferences will never be successful in the way they planned to be. Because once someone has stood up straight and tall, they never again stoop down in quite the same way. And doesn't every slave owner know it!

*Thank you for that reassurance!*

*What do you wish you'd done differently, in your own relationships or even conversations with women?*

*I remember a Northern English playwright admitting once that until the age of 30, the only time he would speak to a woman was "because I fancied her," which doesn't sound like a very balanced way to live.*

Well, remember that England was the successor of much of the ancient world that was hierarchical living personified. A very powerful connection to old Rome. So every class of males would feel entitled that way. Feel that they could reduce women to playthings or nonentities if they wanted. And they'd be completely justified in that, because "that's just how it goes, mate." Natural order of things.

And of course, that's not how it goes. That's how human beings were led to run whole cultures, by instilling fear in half the population, and arrogance and entitlement in the other half. Much easier to control and brainwash a population when you've got them divided against themselves. It's worked for every group of invaders that have ever come to this planet. And for every colonizer invading a "new" continent.

So what I wish I'd done differently, and will do differently in a new Earth life, is to realize that every single human being—regardless of gender, size, color, background, shape, intention—is an expression of Divinity. That there's no one "superior" to anyone else. No one automatically wiser (though children come close!), and no one who automatically ought to rule the roost.

There's no one whose ideas and judgments and opinions weigh heavier and matter more than someone else's, except for when a competent person is facing a decision only they can make. I've supported the hierarchical system in nearly every Earth life I've lived, even those lives I lived as a woman, and definitely the Earth life you speak of, because it supported my preferences and weaknesses, either as a woman needing to go along to get along, or as a guy who needed to be in control.

Some days, that meant control of the creative process, and many days, just control in general.

Because if I wasn't in control, something bad could happen to me or the boys (going back to the Sixties), or to my family, or the music, or my own ego. It was mainly self-preservation, and sometimes, desperation. So I've been learning since leaving a human body to release the need for control, and to allow life to flow through and around me, without needing to shape every moment, without needing a hierarchical or dualistic point of reference. There's a journey for you!

If I were to do it over again, and you don't get the same chance twice, but if I had it to do again, I'd actually listen when women spoke. I'd look to find out what's important to them, and why their interests and needs and requirements differ from men's.

I'd work hard to understand how men and women just don't hear or understand one another for the most part, for most of their lives. And there is brilliant research done in that area, these last 30 years or so, and I strongly recommend that everyone read those books and listen to those talks that explain the breakdowns in communication. What each sex tends to assume about the other, and how they're dead wrong most of the time.

I'd work hard at not putting myself first constantly, and at not expecting the woman to put me first, just because we'd both been trained to think that way by culture or religion or family. I'd never expect good things to happen in any conversation or any moment where I was drunk or high. I wouldn't expect to get my way out of anger, or issuing an edict.

I can tell you, I won't live that way again.

***I'm wondering though, how do women avoid supporting men in their entitlement—how do you dissolve that peacefully, in ways that actually work?***

Well, that's a good question. Because women usually want Peace in the home, and that's a big reason why women have for so long gone along with men's egos. But you also want your own full and complete personhood.

And there will be a clash between those interests some days. At home, on the street, on the train or bus, in a shop, at a job, in the workplace, in a place of worship. What a dreadful phrase, "place of worship." Only a shallow, egotistical god would need to be worshipped! And those are not worth anyone's time.

But I think it takes several things that few girls are taught as they're growing up, and that is to start with, your right to have boundaries. Energetic and emotional boundaries, so that you don't feel responsible for keeping everyone happy all the time. Physical boundaries, so you know it's not OK for a boy or a man to be staring at your body when he should be looking in your eyes as he speaks to you, or grabbing you or making inappropriate comments, whether he's a family member, a stranger, a coworker, boss, teacher—anyone.

## Millions of women are planting a powerful form of higher Light into the center of abuse and exploitation, to uproot and deactivate the whole program.

Growing up I saw the most ridiculous levels of shaming and humiliation heaped on women, even in their own home, just for the fact that they existed. That's how men "made themselves bigger," or so we thought—by making women seem smaller. And of course, that's not real manhood. Yet you see still, to this day, numerous cultures around the world defining themselves by that kind of hierarchy.

That example then gets handed down to the boys in the family, who feel completely vindicated in insulting or degrading their own sisters and mothers, as well as classmates, neighbors, lovers, wives.

There are no rationales where it's OK for the female to take abuse or exploitation, because of the circumstances or the social setting. Some things can be ignored as too trivial to waste energy on. But other things need to be faced and answered, and Stopped.

So after creating boundaries and clear lines (though of course, very young children must be protected), girls must be allowed to use their voices. And that's got to start young. Because most girls, as you know, sort of "lose" their outer voice and their inner courage by the age of 10 or so. They start feeling it's time to fit in, to please, to allow, because if they don't, the right people won't like them. They won't be loved or admired.

That makes room for all kinds of abuse, including letting people convince them to drink more than they feel comfortable drinking, or to try a drug they've never tried, or to go to someone's house where they hardly know anyone. They start taking chances that someone fully declaring their full personhood would never take. Then bad things happen, because there's very nearly no one at home in that young person's body. Particularly if she was abused when younger, she has by then vacated, left her authentic self behind. She is too busy trying to read what other people want of her, trying to be what others prefer.

Unfortunately, there are still people raising their daughters to be pleasing first (no matter what kind of monster is in the room), and true to themselves last. A predator will read that, and completely take over. Having had little to no training in how to assert her rights—she may have been raised to think she has none—the girl will freeze in a situation of physical or sexual assault, rather than do all she can to stop it happening to her or a friend. She'll often then suppress the memory, though the trauma will continue to affect her for years to come. Then when those memories do rise to the surface, they're overwhelming.

*Yes. It can take years to overcome the post-traumatic stress disorder from abuse. Even after the most involved levels of healing, some of it always remains with you.*

*From infancy, I had no idea I had rights. Even as a young adult, I was utterly without boundaries, which opens you up to ongoing abuse from a raft of people.*

*I had to go through a whole process in therapy to learn how to create real boundaries. Then I had to learn about etheric boundaries.*

*Often a daughter is raised to accept abuse because there's the belief that certain men, especially the men in their family, could never do wrong. And the child's mother lacks the wherewithal to see what's happening, or to stop it if she does see it.*

*It's a form of "all maleness is sacred." It's a huge matrix. You go along with it, because you're too weakened from the abuse to know any different. And then one day you notice what a hell your life is—abusive jobs, bosses, relationships, total lack of fulfillment—and you decide to break the very rules you were told made you acceptable.*

This is exactly the scenario you came in to live out. You and millions of other women are planting a powerful form of higher Light into the center of that abuse and exploitation, to begin to uproot and deactivate the whole program.

And it is a program, you're right. None of it is accidental. The old power crowd, as you call them, have a whole technological and etheric system set up to feed off of the horror of women and children who undergo abuse. And that abuse can happen anywhere, to anyone.

This is why nearly all of those institutions support exactly what you're describing. They set out to destroy the God Within— the Divine in human form.

And who better to exemplify that, than the women of the world, who themselves are capable of bringing forth new life?

So, OK—we've talked about girls creating strong boundaries, and about females being taught to use their voice from a young age, without censoring themselves, though obviously young children are always quite vulnerable.

I would add to that, that all cultures must now admit that the Divine Feminine exists, and that the powers of the Feminine be acknowledged and honored. These include bridge-building, communication, relationship-forming, invention and design, ideas creation. The repression of those gifts is something the world has suffered from for thousands of years.

The incredibly beautiful thing, is that we see all of these powerful shifts coming forward now, even on the days when they appear not to be. Even when you have a so-called world leader or two making insulting comments about women and bragging about having assaulted them, while those who vote for those men protect and support them. The higher Light now reaching the planet and the awakening consciousness of the human race cannot be stopped.

You have made your decision collectively, as a race. You are moving into the fifth dimensional forms of life in which all persons are viewed as equal in worth. Of course that can't happen overnight. But it is unfolding, and you're already adjusting to it.

Yet the more you rejoice in that—the more you *expect* it— the faster and more joyfully it happens.

***Are you able to assist us, you and all who are on your level etherically, watching us from the higher realms?***

***To send us Light and energy waves that spur us on, keep us from being discouraged, remind us this is part of what we came here for?***

Of course! I do what I can, within the boundaries of Universal Law. Nearly all of us do. There are varying degrees of involvement. Some etheric beings stand well back and observe, assisting with their objectivity. They "hold space" for your fifth dimensional Earth visions, you might say. Others see the probable outcomes and decide no immediate assistance is required. Yet their assumption of victory for humanity assists the energy waves empowering you.

Others roll up their sleeves and help nonstop, however they can. Others work more intermittently, according to their particular role or mission. But we are all rooting for you, all of us in the Light. Ready to lend our wisdom whenever asked to do so.

One more thing to add, though I could probably go on from here to add even more. But I'll just say, that to encourage girls and young women, and really, all young people, to use their creative gifts in whatever form is most joyful for them, is one of the best possible ways to assist anyone in inheriting their full Divinity, and their full humanity.

That, and letting boys know as they grow up that all persons are to be loved and respected, that they are not here to rule the

Earth, and that their feminine aspect is dying to express itself—and that they squash and deny that at their peril.

All of that, utterly vital, utterly needed. At all times!

How can you only be half a human? Mainly Masculine in orientation (regardless of your outer shape) and not fully aware, even, of the power of the Feminine? You lose yourself in that process. If I could, I would beg humanity to stop throwing half their power, inventiveness, brilliance, and staying power into the fire.

Claim who you are! A creating god/goddess. Someone worth being. Someone worth celebrating!

# 9

# A Holographic Universe

*How do we deal with the darkness and desperation we see now in the world? Wars and refugee situations, human trafficking, immigrants (including thousands of children) held in concentration camps all over the US, environmental protections being rolled back to allow fracking and drilling on sacred lands, the pandemic, 5G, to name just a few.*

*How do we deal with having to face the depths of duality, yet still move out of it?*

*Is the old power crowd trying to push us into despair with all these images? To keep reaping our low vibrational emotional energy to keep their matrix machinery going, even though they know they're finished?*

Of course that's part of it. There are a number of working components here. I can explain a few things so that you can become more objective about what you see happening in the world.

First of all, your higher self doesn't get upset at what you call injustices.

Higher selves almost always see the long range purpose and potential outcomes of Earth situations, even the conundrums that humankind lives with all the time. Higher selves don't rage or get worried or upset, because they view outer events as temporarily fleshed out ideas, not permanent realities.

Unlike your Earth self, your higher self engages with these illusions (and that's what they are) on a whole other level. A higher self knows that while emotion is a powerful manifestation tool, it can also present huge pitfalls. They remain neutral and stabilized.

It's very easy to view a horrible scene on television or read about it on the internet, and conclude all is lost. You're still in a human body. So your energies are already resonating with the trauma experienced in this and other lives. That trauma rings out like a bell and resonates with everything on that frequency. Then all the effects get compounded, and life feels hopeless.

Be aware that your discussions of world events actually powerfully serve to reshape those situations, even if you think you're only *commenting* on what you're seeing, with no hope of influencing it. That is true for your own life situations as well.

You all increasingly hold powerful influence. Particularly when you see something happening and feel strongly that things shouldn't go that way. *The energies coming in now are such that they support your awareness on all levels.* So that when you see something you would love to improve, just get that improved state into your mind. Picture that improvement clearly, and back it up with strong desire. In that moment, that improved situation begins to develop, even if you think it's stuck fast in desperation mode.

That's how powerful your words and images are, and that equally applies to your own life situations. You truly are co-Creators that way. For too long, people have felt that Divinity was far down the road somewhere—out in the Universe where they couldn't reach it. Or that it was so powerful that if they did step onto that holy ground, they'd be reduced to dust.

That's an image given you by organized religion, and it's funny that they don't call it organized crime religion, because the two worlds are powerfully connected. Watch the third installment of the *Godfather* movies if you doubt that one. (Though it's true of all major religions, not just Catholicism.)

*And yet there's still a real time gap between our viewing what we feel is an awful injustice, and an improvement in that situation. Plenty of people image the positive. Yet there are still wars raging. The glaciers are still melting. Children are still getting trafficked or being sent to immigration prisons, despite the hard work and prayers of so many good-hearted people.*

*What do we do about it? Stay home and envision a better world?*

You've been given strict instruction—and here's the Masculine dominance program again—that outer action is the only kind that counts. And it does have its place. It can be great at solving problems, no question. But taking inner action first, particularly for the long range problems you describe, will save you many weeks and months of ineffectual or misguided action.

When you envision a possible solution, you enter the quantum field, as some people call it—the realm of all possibilities.

In that wide open field, you can try out different solutions and ideas. You can see which ones seem to answer all aspects of the situation, and which ones ring true with your own inner compass about the higher good.

If the first thing you want to do is get children out of prisons and into situations where they receive the help, safety, and support they need, that has to be envisioned first.

Parallel to that is envisioning the arrests and convictions of the ones who decided to profit off of children being in prisons and concentration camps, and sold to pedophile rings and the like. Maybe the third point would be to expel from all branches of government and law enforcement all those who covered up those crimes, and all those who supported, enabled, or took part in them. And you want to begin right now building a world where those kinds of criminal actions are never repeated, anywhere.

**You have stepped in at this time to play your last third dimensional Earth role, in ways that will expand your soul knowledge and power to levels you only ever dreamt of before now.**

Immediately that you hear this, your logical left brain is going to cry out, "But *how* do we do all of that? These people run the world! They hold the reins of power." The logical mind will demand answers on that front. Except that you haven't got any yet.

And let me tell you, that demand for "How" is what slows or stops most of the positive manifestations in the world. You've been purposefully trained to think in a show-me-the-money masculine way of doing things, so you'll get caught up in the How. Then the thing itself, the great Change you've been advocating for, gets stuck in the pipeline and can't show up.

*You don't need to know How.* Especially when How is still being formed. You only need to know that your higher self will figure out the details, so long as you continue to image the changes, the beautiful outcomes. That process has got nothing to do with, "I have to know every step along the way."

Those steps are still being created! Much of it is still pure energy, forming and starting to take shape. Just specify that it all come forward in ways that are for the higher good of everyone involved. That's all you have to do. The dreaming, the envisioning of the end result, your delight in that, your *expectation* of it, is your point of creation.

All of you manifest this way all the time, though you don't realize it. You picture something and back it up with feelings of happiness, Joy, relief—till one day it comes to you. And that's because you held unwavering focus on the thing itself. Joy is a powerful element to the process, because that says to the Universe, "It's already here—I can feel it!"

And the Universe, accepting that frequency ringing out powerfully from your being, is bound by Universal Law to say Yes to that. It is bound to produce the very hologram that cures and reverses the one that made you suffer.

It's got nothing to do with how evil this politician or that oil baron is. It looks like they're the problem. They're not. They're just helping to provide you with the kind of dense, shadowy experience you came here to learn from.

You're on a stage playing a role, and so are they. That curtain will fall—believe me, believe all of us, when we say, *The curtain is already falling on the old Earth.* You're already stepping out of your Victim role, just as they're coming out of their Predator role. That's what time it is.

The new era is born. The planets have decided that. You have decided that. And you have stepped in at this particular time to honor that timing. And to play your last third dimensional Earth role in ways that will stretch and expand your soul knowledge and power to levels you only ever dreamt of before now.

Is that easy or preferable? No, of course not. But you didn't come here to be comfortable. Unless you want to birth a comfortable life. And by that I don't mean a life where you have great wealth, perfect health, and joyful relationships, and face only the tiniest challenges as you sail round the Hawaiian islands. That is not your path at present. That kind of enjoyment and easygoing pace *can* be your path, but it's not what most of you decided to experience right now.

Whatever you envision for yourself, you can write that into your story, your life path, even as you're living it. Use the method of taking time each day to envision and fully *feel* the reality of what you desire. You can do that. Of course you can. But you will still see the pain, the shock, the unbelievable suffering of others on this Earth, and desire to heal and to help. That's just who you are, all of you hearing me now with an open heart. So you can still get emotionally pulled in and manipulated, and you need to be aware of that.

And I can tell you, all this talk about "oust this regime" or "throw that one out of office" and "arrest this one and his friends, and then we'll be free of all this madness" as the first remedy to establish just doesn't cut it. The same overhanging structure—the same inherent power games—would still be in place, with those puppets replaced by new ones.

I didn't fully understand that in Earth life, but I understand it now. You don't actually see the face or know the names of the ones in charge. They are well hidden. Some in bases and installations deep within the Earth herself, others afloat on some space station somewhere, trying to avoid arrest or other complications, because they know their time is up.

There's no one date by which time the planet will be free of the descendants and accomplices of the invaders who came to the Earth so long ago. As you increasingly leave Time behind on this planet—as Time moves increasingly faster, and the linear way of viewing Time fades, it all becomes a moot point anyway.

Now is the only time that exists, and the only one you ever need.

*You're describing a holographic Universe that is similar to a computer program. What you create in the quantum field, you eventually see happening around you.*

*And within that, all of us on Earth who are outside the planetary power structure have been subject to a matrix full of programs, created specifically to keep us under strict control. Disempowered for millennia.*

*So are you saying now that our imaginations and heart-mind can create other programs that rewrite what we've been handed by our "overlords"? Is that our way out?*

Yes, I am. But that's not your only way out. You don't really need a way out. You need to realize that this is a multidimensional world. It always was, but you're aware of it now. And that makes all the difference.

You all need to understand that you were never so disempowered as you've assumed. What you feel and hold in your heart-mind to be true is what you experience, always. And you do have a lot of control over that. Over the *quality* of your experience. Over how you *receive* and *perceive* what's happening around you.

So let's say I'm back on Earth, only this time they don't shoot me—they find a reason to throw me into prison for decades.

Even in that prison, I can still remember the feeling of being out in Nature. I can recall the sight, sound, and smell of the sea. I can recall a busy street or a child's face. I can hold close the presence of loved ones in my thoughts and feelings. I can live and breathe in the present moment. I can consider all of *that* my reality—the beauty of life, not the desperation of it—even while physically inside grim circumstances.

Now here's the odd part: as illogical as that behavior would be—and it's an active choice, not a reaction—it would actually start to shape my everyday life after a while. I would either be freed in time, if that's all I felt and affirmed was real for me, or I would be moved to a less oppressive form of imprisonment. Or I would find a lot of freedom in the meaning of everyday life there. At the very least, my outer experience would lighten in some way.

You are also imprisoned, but only in part. Every time you assert your freedom by imaging a safe, beautiful, peaceful world where every child is safe and well-cared for, and every person respected and honored, and feel real thankfulness for that, you help to create that. You literally begin to walk into the reality of what you are envisioning, and will start to feel the realness of it, even before it starts to show up outwardly.

*No one* can take that reality from you. It is yours. It is your creation. It is yours to experience, regardless of other influences. And as you experience it, even if only for yourself, you spread the news energetically that *everyone on Earth can create this new form of life as a collective reality.*

This goes very far beyond the positive affirmation or positive thinking you've heard so much about, though those ideas are on the right track. I would say, those things are great if you can feel the reality of them. At that point, you've thrown a new image up on the blank screen, and you start to resonate with that. It's a point of focus. If you can hold your focus fully enough, the Universe then begins to crank out the outer experience of that.

**You're not really made to carry the weight of hundreds or thousands of other souls on your back.**

But when those affirmations go against what you believe deep down to actually exist—to be "true"—then they have little effect. Your carefully controlled subconscious would still win every time, assuring your conscious mind, "that can't happen." It then blocks the manifestation.

This is why spiritually aware people are so much knocked about by life. They have their beautiful desires for health, wealth, fulfillment, a chance to serve others in fulfilling ways. Yet they don't see the outcomes they desire because they're subconsciously stuck in some program that says, "You don't have choices. Just do as you're told." Or "You're not worthy of that."

Notice how the New Age spirituality as they call it has been shaped into a kind of religion. And how its followers often fall into the same rut of dogma and correctness as those who have for millennia followed traditional religions, when people called out to the God of the heavens in distress, and felt they were never answered. Same situation, different day. This time you're asking "the Universe" for an Answer, and not always hearing it.

From where I stand now, we would say that the answer comes without your being aware of it. It's not necessarily the answer you're looking for. It's the one you resonate with energetically. The answer you've received is, "You are where you are because that is your wavelength. That is what you exude. What you ask for is stuck in a no-go area, because you have accidentally placed it in the category of Not Here Yet, or Not Sure I Deserve It. Or Not Convinced the Universe Has My Back." So there it sits.

A person's sensitivity can present another pitfall. However necessary that gift is to your life path, it does hold you back at times. You carry numerous energetic interferences (people, memories, imprints) with you in life, and that is exhausting. You're not really made to carry the weight of hundreds or thousands of other souls on your back. That is not your job, and they must be cleared out, and new intruders kept out from inhabiting your energies.

Most Light Bringers also carry the pains and trauma of their family, ancestors, culture, religion, gender, ethnicity, and so on. Most families wait centuries for the right Light Being, a natural healer, to enter their circle, to heal and restore them to wholeness. Yet that is also not your job, and you have to, at least telepathically, tell your family and ancestors that. Expel the weight of their presence from your own energies. It's too much.

## Your life won't make sense while you're trying to squash it into the old, narrow categories. Your energies are too powerful for that.

Most people need help with this, and there are excellent energy workers available to help you, nor does it always cost a great deal to get that help. This is another psychological/energy block that is a very old trap—the belief that you may need this or that kind of help, but never have the money to pay for it. If you just image yourself getting that energy work done and benefiting from it powerfully, the way will be paved toward that, and often more quickly than you'd think.

So stop playing by the old rules! They really don't apply anymore. Your life won't make sense while you're trying to squash it into the old, narrow categories of thinking, feeling, doing. Your energies are growing too powerful for that.

Now is the time to break the old rules. I almost want to beg people to start thinking in terms of all the potentials open to them now, rather than reverting to the old, "That sort of thing never happens for me" or "It's so hard to create more money" or "I always hate my day job" or "I'm always in need" or "I would feel funny accepting all that just for myself." Or "It's just a crazy world—nothing you can do about it."

These are simply old programs, designed to keep you small. But are you small now, really? Aren't you as big as the energies and intentions that create whole worlds? Aren't you as tall and strong and resourceful as the greatest magicians and alchemists?

The only difference between you and them, is that they know how powerful they are. And they don't waste time apologizing for it.

So the next time you want to remake your world, and you're looking for a leader—the right ascended master or off-world being—look in the mirror.

*There's* the one you hoped would finally land—the Star Being with amazing ability to transform life on Earth.

# 10

# Imagine

*In an earlier chapter, you spoke of returning to a new Earth life. What sort of a life would that be, do you think?*

*Would you return to the Western world? Would you choose not to be so well-known this time? Will you still be an artist and a musician?*

*Keep in mind that millions will feel disappointed if you say No to that last question, but no pressure . . .*

I'm not new to the pressures of what millions of people want from me! It was a way of life for a while there. An unhappy one, when my own instincts veered well away from what industry execs or fans wanted from me. And you'll note I broke out of that at one point in a big way. So none of that comes into play. I've experienced it. I'm done.

The details of the next life have not been fully formulated yet. I will play music again, but in what way and who with—that's still being written. I've been a musician in a number of lives. Most of them, not well known, or at least not during that lifetime.

The pressures involved in high-level fame are such that they can pull you off your path, and it takes tremendous inner resolve to stay on it. You've seen a lot of casualties in the music business since you were quite young. Everyone has. So you know what I'm talking about there.

**Why are so many people in the music industry killed? And then their deaths covered up as an overdose, or an accident or an illness. What's the reason? They weren't following the power crowd's orders?**

That's one reason. Sometimes they just demand too much, and threaten those in control that they'll expose them if they don't get what they want. Now, sometimes that actually works, to a point. But I made up my mind pretty early on that I wasn't going to chance it. I saw some people go down for that.

But more likely, the performer was falling apart from drugs or drinking, and they weren't producing as required anymore. Or they wanted total artistic control, which is granted to very few people. Or were ready to release information and insights that those in power wanted to keep quiet.

Some think they're indestructible, and can do whatever they want—that those in power owe them because of all the money they've made for those in control. Of course, those in power don't see it that way. They just get rid of them. Sometimes they clone them first, and program the clone to do as it's told. Problem solved, or so they think.

**I can hear a lot of people right now saying, "You can't clone a human! You can only clone a sheep!" Which is kind of funny, when you think about it. (I always say, "If they can clone one mammal, they can clone another.")**

**You lost a lot of friends in the Sixties and Seventies. Some of your closest friends. And I'm wondering if most of the famous or near-famous ones were taken down one way or another because they had become a nuisance politically—too much influence, like yourself. Or they were asking questions about things that someone didn't want them looking into.**

***Some did get replaced by a clone or something similar—someone who would carry out the power crowd's objectives in the way they preferred.***

For those working on that level, it's not hard to create an accident or an overdose, or even a serious illness. That has happened all over the place, for a very long time. The losses we saw in the Sixties and Seventies cost many survivors some of our *own* life energy, even. Because when you're connected to someone on a heart level—and I didn't understand this at the time—and they leave the Earth suddenly or violently, a part of you can travel off with them. The part that refuses to let go. And some of their energy remains with you.

It's important to let go of people after they pass, or after they're no longer in your life. It won't happen immediately, but it must happen. Because to live fully, to have full presence and awareness on this Earth, you need all of you present. That's difficult for those who suffered trauma at an early age, I realize. You don't want to fully live in the body. But it's important to focus on grounding yourself and being fully present. You miss a lot of your own life energy otherwise. You miss the present moment, the only thing that really exists.

For years in the late Sixties and into the Seventies, I wasn't fully present. Yoko's spirit and presence kept me grounded in ways that other things couldn't. Obviously the drugs and the drinking didn't help. When you hear the lyric "it's all too much," it's partly a reference to how much went down in that era—for me, and for everyone at that time. The drugs opened up whole aspects of my psyche I wasn't ready for, though that was only part of it. It really was too much. Life was spinning out of control. The loss of loved ones was a part of that.

And yes, they've replaced people in various ways. That still happens. Sometimes, it's the people you call White Knights replacing someone with a clone and hiding the original person, for their own safety. Someone well-known, an influencer who's gone against the grain in their actions, statements, or intentions. Not unusual.

*In this next Earth life, will you again help people to awaken, to realize their true selves? Remind them that they came in for a reason?*

I hope I'm doing that now! Right now as you bring my words to the page, and always. I work with anyone who is open to working with me, whether it's for music or visual art, or bringing in higher energies in ways that help reshape Earth systems and Earth thought into new paradigms. New patterns and inventions that lift things to a higher frequency.

So while I'm not an ascended master who ascended during an Earth life, I am a guide and support to those who desire to evoke change and move life to a higher level. There are millions of us—more than you could count. It's just Earth's own thick atmosphere energetically that keeps people from seeing how well-loved and supported they are. Keeps them thinking they're alone in what they're facing. Nothing could be further from the truth.

Where we begin as guides and helpers, whether you're on the Earth now or not, isn't "the Earth's in trouble and needs rescuing!" It's more, "How do we envision life so as to create Peace everywhere? What needs to resonate in us, in order to help create the New Human? What needs to happen so cultures work together in Peace? So that the old situations get pulled out of chaos, into new and higher forms?"

For some of that, higher technologies are needed. Because there is a lot of detoxification and cleansing of the Earth that needs to happen. Both physical and energetic. Some of that is already happening, because there are people from elsewhere in this Universe who have come to Earth specifically to assist the planet now. And many beautiful Light beings in human form are assisting there as well.

Animals, plant life, and humans also need complete detoxification, but first we work with the air, soil, water, rocks, minerals. All that's suffered interferences such as mining, fracking, and nuclear contamination, and needs badly to be healed. So that comes down the line first, even as healing technologies for Earth beings start to come on line.

And yes, it's time for people to know their true selves. It's impossible to leave that out. You start by no longer squashing those inner feelings you get that warn you that something is not right for you, or not necessary. Time to notice that and heed it. And to notice when you get the feeling that something *is* right for you. That you need to look into that more, or take a chance and say "Yes" to it.

Too many people ignore those feelings, because they've been trained to. So they shove aside their true selves in favor of living out a self that's been manufactured. That self is not who they really are. It took me years to throw off the false self. I was only just managing to start being my authentic self—the self who was not an addict or an abuser or a famous guy, but a simple and aware human being—when I got pulled out of Earth life.

It can take decades to know who you really are, but this is one of the greatest journeys a human being can go on. And you have now the advantage of energy workers who can assist you in healing the fractured aspects of spirit and psyche, and who can chase out of your energies the influences and presences that shouldn't be there. People think, "That's just who I am," yet it isn't.

The era you're in now is a miracle compared to even 60 years ago, when these ideas were still new and laughed at.

Anyone seeking to know their true self has to begin asking themselves what is really joyful and fun and easy for them. What really resonates with them. What feels lightest and best to them. That's not hard, except that most people only ever bump into their true selves by accident. Then they might laugh it off, or they're embarrassed to admit "that's who I really am," because they grew up hearing, "That's not a good thing to be," or "You'll never make any money at that."

Yes, of course you need money. What's interesting is that in the developed world, more people die of misery—high blood pressure, heart disease, cancer, addictions, depression—than die of starvation. If I had to choose, I'd go hungry more often just so I could live my real life and feel joyful more often, if it came to that.

Thankfully, you don't have to choose anymore. You've got a whole international market open to you through the internet, and nearly anyone can start their own independent work or their own business these days, to do what you love, or to sustain yourself while you do what makes you joyful. Granted, that's not the answer for everyone. But it's a start.

*Our economic system has folded up and collapsed, worldwide, mainly orchestrated by the powers-that-were. They want us to despair, to feel trampled, to just give up. Is that the whole idea? Or is there something else as well?*

*Because it's not working for them to put us in such a bad state. It's created more intervention from higher beings and galactic beings. It's created more active awareness, not less.*

Well, it does look grim at the minute, if you're looking at the numbers. But then the numbers were always an illusion. The outcome was designed to bring wholesale despair, yes. A collective giving up, so that people would accept any solution as the antidote.

When in fact, as you say, it's woken people up. It's told them, "This system has *never* really worked. It was designed to sustain and reward the millionaires and billionaires, the corporations, the elite .01%, while the working man and woman grow smaller and smaller in size and significance."

They are trying to downgrade your minds, your bodies, and your spiritual awareness down to the level of a trained chimp. And yes, that program has been in place for a long time.

But the acceleration of it in this era means that they know they are out of time.

## Humanity is beginning to live first in spirit, and second in the body, ascending beyond the forms that have enslaved you for millennia.

The Light coming into the planet now—into all living things, all consciousness, all systems, all awareness—has shifted the balance in favor of Life over technology, however impressive that technology might seem at times.

Starting around 60 years ago, a steady social, political, economic downturn was created to lower the vibration of the masses, so that they would accept any seeming relief, any political "solution" offered them. You see the results of that now.

There are other reasons as well. There are in numerous parts of the world, powerful energy points in the land itself that when activated, influence the world in many ways. This means that the counter influence to all this madness is a powerful one. It's one that the powers-that-were didn't fully bank on. And that's that Light Beings in human form are working with the power spots on the Earth, magnifying the power of those places for positive outcomes.

You don't have to physically live near any of the sacred lands to tap into their powerful energy currents and direct them to create positive outcomes. You can go there etherically, in meditation or in sleep. You all travel out-of-body, in spirit form, as you sleep at night. Nearly all of you wander to various places on the Earth, as well as to other planets and stars, ships, and dimensions, to do your work. You even visit other timelines.

The power spots are awake and alive with mysteries that are so old, they well pre-date the Earth, because so many of them come from etheric or off-planet sources and cultures. Some of them are pyramids that have many chambers and underground corridors hidden from those who don't know how to access them.

Some of these power points have underground cities built into them. Others are ancient forests, or have underground laboratories, libraries, or starships. Others are crystal gardens. Many look to be just plain open expanses of Nature. Yet the energies that emanate from them, and the intergalactic communications taking place via their energy lines, are astounding.

Though the powers-that-were have tried to hide, destroy, or use these locations for their own purposes, they have been unsuccessful for the most part.

And this is the interesting part: These old families, the old bloodlines that long ago appointed themselves rulers of the planet, are falling apart rapidly now, due to degradation of their bodies and minds, in addition to their frantic infighting and financial collapse. Those aware of the hierarchy and its true nature and construct often imagine they're in a battle or a great war of some sort, in which they are spreading Light as a sort of weapon against the dark.

What humanity is coming into is actually the release of all that. The release of good/bad or Light/dark duality we spoke of earlier. It's time to stop naming enemies. It's time to go beyond that. I had a glimpse of that world when I wrote "Imagine."

And it's true what people say, that if Yoko hadn't been the kind of artist she is, asking people to use the right-brain function of valuing symbols and ideals, and the possibilities that the imagination offers, that song could never have been written.

We were literally going beyond the boundaries of countries, of education, of cultures, of religions, of nationalities. It was a glimpse into people being finally free.

I didn't admit that while I was on the Earth—that I owed much of that song to Yoko's influence. I gladly admit it now. I have no use for ego and ownership any longer. Not of a song or a person or a reputation. Humanity is also growing beyond that, but the difference is, people are beginning to do that while still in a body! That's the miracle of it.

Humanity is beginning to live first in spirit, and second in the body. Ascending beyond the forms that have enslaved you for millennia.

Yes, I know things look quite troubled, yet what a moment! What an astounding, amazing, unprecedented time to be alive.

# 11

# Earth Life Complications

*Are you sorry, in that case, that you're no longer here with us?*

*I was watching the video for "Mind Games" the other day, and again was sad that you are no longer on the Earth. Your presence was much needed, then and now.*

I was bothered for some time after leaving the Earth, that I left the way I did, and when I did. And so suddenly. It threw off a lot of people's energy, and not just the loved ones who knew me personally.

I somewhat said good-bye inwardly to those I loved before I left, but they couldn't hear that, of course. I have whispered it to them in their sleep, so they have received it, subconsciously at least. They know it's there.

What was most disturbing was leaving two children behind. Particularly as one was still quite small, and I knew he still needed me. The soul will make decisions sometimes on our behalf, and what's called an untimely death can be one of those decisions. Sometimes our work is best done in energy form, with us out of the body, not in it. So I was pulled out of that Earth life, despite my objections.

I haven't always agreed with my soul's decisions, and have told it as much. Nearly everyone's soul has done things they don't like or approve of. The higher self can also be outvoted—people do that all the time—and clearly, so can the Earth self. There are various ways to ensure that that kind of sudden disruption doesn't happen again, but much soul healing and reintegration must take place first.

Otherwise, we're on a track that travels down the road and takes us along, with or without our agreement.

### Are our lives that out of control—out of synch with our spirit and our essence?

Yes and no. Much depends on your history and your current path. It depends on your soul history, your soul path and mission, and your higher self's strength and determination not to be overridden. And how much power you ascribe to this or that aspect of your consciousness. Or to your Divine aspect.

You have to understand that we've all experienced more fracturing, more trauma, and more interferences energetically than we'd like to think. Few people face that fully while in a body, and many refuse to see it even once they rejoin the etheric. It's not an easy path, because if you spend time on the Earth, you're subject to so many interferences, so much chaos and violence, so many juxtaposing intentions (many of them your own), that confusion can result. A confusion of identity, of resources, of ability, of soul path.

Not easy to explain in ways people will grasp, as your conditioning goes straight against it. Religion has a lot riding on your not seeing the complications of Earth life. Not seeing how past lives control whole aspects of your psyche, because of buried trauma. Not seeing how your ancestors hover around you and can protect you or impede your progress many days, according to what they think is best. Not seeing how some Spirit guides are not always up to certain tasks.

And not seeing how many darker beings or lost spirits are floating through the atmosphere, looking for an empty vessel—someone who has a body but whose consciousness is "rarely at home"—so they can move in and influence or control that Earth life like it was their own.

Religions would prefer you follow the old "Do as we say and you'll be OK" idea. Which has never worked. There is no one set of beliefs that ensures everything will be OK, on Earth or after it. Except maybe, "I know that if I remain as honest and conscious as possible with myself about what requires integration, healing, and evolvement, I can create that for myself, if I'm willing to walk the path. If I'm willing to keep moving into higher levels of Light." And that's more an inner Knowing, not a belief program.

That probably comes the closest of any of it, yet even that doesn't quite cover it.

There's always more to learn! You don't suddenly arrive on the Other Side one day, and suddenly all is forgotten and forgiven. Of a sudden, you're a joyful little Angel floating around humming happily.

You've got questions. You've got healing that needs to happen. And you've still got plenty to learn, which anyone can figure out after viewing their life events. That's a sort of fast-moving flow of images of the Earth life you just left. You view it after being in the etheric long enough to have rebalanced your energies, and are ready to review the life you've just experienced.

And it's enlightening! You see the results of everything you did, thought, felt, and spoke. The results on your own life, and on those around you. You feel what they felt, as well as what you felt at the time.

*From what I understand from shamanic friends and energy workers, if someone expects to end up in a beautiful place where everyone is joyful and fulfilled and "singing God's praises" as they say, they will find themselves experiencing just that.*

*If they expect to end up in a purgatory or a hell, or a blank nothingness, then that will happen, because the Other Side is all about projected thought. If you believe it and expect it, it appears before you. That seems to be what people see in near death experiences. Their personal beliefs are demonstrated, played out right in front of them.*

*Have you found that that's so? It really is a holographic Universe, in that case.*

Well, it's even more intense than that! Not in a bad way, just in a very real way. You do project outwardly your own expectations, to a good degree. You must also face the outcome of your Earthly creations. And that includes your belief systems, which in general can be very confining.

Belief systems try to tell you who you are. They describe who their particular god is, and who you and that god are to each other. They use only so many words and culturally directed meanings to do that. Yet things are plenty bigger than that. Bigger than any one philosophy or religion. Bigger than any one spiritual teacher or artist could ever explain.

So whatever "they" told you, I can tell you, that's way, way too small. Too small to do justice to this Universe and your own consciousness.

*So what kind of healing needs to happen?*

That will depend on how much and what kind of trauma you've been carrying. That unresolved pain and shock will be the aggregate of all your lives on Earth and other planets and dimensions, as well as the trauma you experienced in the life you just left. People don't realize how much they carry with them.

It's why you meet people who seem to have a good life—a good income, a spouse who loves them, bright and healthy children, a nice home—yet they're never happy, never in a good way with life.

They are literally being chased down by elements of their current life and all their other lives, without realizing it. Their subconscious is letting out a low howl of pain, and they express that accidentally in every word and action. They can't tell you what's wrong. *They* don't know what's wrong. They haven't got that information.

This is why I found it helpful to scream out my pain and frustration at life, and my grief, which often reduced to rage, when I got into therapy in the Seventies. People thought it was ridiculous, that kind of therapy, but it was what I needed to do. It's what a lot of people need to do. Because without some physical action that involves the heart's energies and expels the rage that comes from seeing and experiencing suffering on this planet—without that outlet, you can be a bit of loose cannon, energetically.

You don't need to scream—you can beat a drum or practice yoga or just cry, or write out whatever energies you're carrying. But it has to come forward in order to be healed.

Everyone is also born with what are called psychic abilities, which are actually very natural abilities, not a mysterious "sixth sense." It's just a person's energetic nature. Everyone's had an intuitive feeling that warned them not to go to a particular place at a particular time. Or that encouraged them to take a chance on something that their rational thinking told them was nonsense.

Yet they find, after acting on that inner push, that something wonderful results from it. Or they find out later that by taking a different route to work than usual, they avoided being in a serious accident. And they can't tell you why they made that decision.

People might even be thankful for those intuitive moments. And yet they rarely ask themselves, "What else is going on that I don't know about? What else is working on me, affecting me, calling out a warning or an encouragement, that I don't hear because I've closed off from it?"

As I've said elsewhere, children and animals—babies especially—are highly aware and not easily fooled. Yet children reach an age where they start to believe the lies they're hearing around them. Because if they don't believe it, it means that their family, who mean everything to them, aren't right all the time. Or maybe don't love them enough to tell them the truth.

The thought of that is too terrible. So they shut off most of their intuitive abilities, so they can believe what they're told, and belong to their family and community. Meanwhile, their higher aspect is saying, "Some of this is wrong for *me*, and some of it is just Wrong for anyone." That flashing red light is warning them to detach from what they're seeing and hearing. But that's too hard to do when you're young and need to be nourished and accepted. They also carry their parents' DNA and ancestral and family patterns, and those influences are too powerful to calculate. They handle the subconscious like a set of controls.

They're also stuck in a powerful energetic web that's covered the planet for millennia, that tells people how to think and feel. It takes years to even become aware of that web, let alone disengage from it.

Most people live in denial about all this, and that's OK. At least part of the time, it protects people from remembering abuse episodes till they're strong enough to handle it. It gives them the opportunity to live out the beliefs and the culture they chose to come into, to learn new things, to resolve things that happened in other lives.

Yet sooner or later, the true self demands to be heard.

## Your gifts, your true passion, are not a side show!

I'm going to say that for most people, in most eras on the Earth, that process of connecting to the true self was not going to happen while they were in a body. Most people have worn the makeup and costume of their particular life role fully, as if it defined them. Most have just tried to survive.

Then their spirits left their body at the end of it all, and they were sort of, "Oh, wait. That wasn't me! That was just the era, the culture, the body, the family I chose to be born into. My true self stood on the sidelines and just watched. I held them off. Next life, I will determine to be who I really am."

And do they make it? Sometimes. Even a strong-willed stubborn ass like myself, in my last Earth life, doesn't always come clean about who they really are and what they're really on

Earth to do. So many of us are so terrified of not looking "man" enough, or not being the "kind" of woman we think we ought to be, that we build up all kinds of invisible barriers that even we can barely see past.

Then if a friend says to us, "Why aren't you working as an artist? Your work is amazing," or "Why aren't you working as a healer? That seems to be your real gift," we get all shy and confused or think we're being modest by denying our true calling, and saying, "I can't, for practical reasons."

Complete nonsense. Your gifts, your true passion, are not a side show! That's center stage. It's why you came in. There's a ton of growth to be had, in overcoming family and cultural objection to the true self. Worse yet are our own objections. Just ridiculous. There's always some hour in the day when you can admit to your true passions, and live that out. Live from your soul and higher aspect.

I didn't have a lot of trouble overcoming other people's objections to my being an artist, because I didn't feel I had a family in the narrow sense of the term. And the culture I was born into didn't think I'd amount to much anyway. So art school was not much of a shock to the people around me, and neither was my playing music. I ignored whatever opposition there was.

When I was younger, my driving force, though I didn't know it at the time, was to say that art and music are not just amusements. They're powerful statements that affect and empower everyday life. That was a challenge, because so many still view any art form as fluff or entertainment, not the blood that runs through the veins of a civilization. Not Truth trying to be seen.

I had my work cut out in that respect. From there, I had no choice but to face my true self. Having a child can also make you face yourself.

So I would say, once you've transitioned back into the etheric as they call it, the healing you're offered is to heal your fractured inner self. The self who got destroyed or at least badly impaired by punishments, corrections, abuse, poverty, mass mind control, trauma, imprisonment of one kind or another, heavy emotion, illness or injury, neglect.

Some of that starts in childhood and continues on, like a pattern that keeps automatically repeating. Some of it develops later. It's compounded, because you've experienced those situations in so many lifetimes, and those experiences collect. They don't fade behind you in the mist like people assume.

The split between the real self and the falsely created, injured one has to be mended. So upon reaching the Other Side, most people don't suddenly rejoin higher dimensional life. They are first cared for and nurtured—put into a kind of restful sleep. Then while they're resting, their consciousness is helped to integrate past experiences, without retaining the shock and pain of them, though there's still more learning to be done.

Often people will still have questions—"Could I have done more for this son or daughter?" Or "How do I apologize to my spouse or partner who's still on the Earth, because I wasn't faithful (or kind or patient enough)?" Or "I came in to be a healer (or a builder or a warrior, etc.) but I completely sidestepped that."

Or "I knew what was happening. I knew they were arresting people of that faith (or color, or political bent, or nationality), and I did nothing. How do I make up for that?"

People have so many questions, I couldn't begin to list them all.

So we attend what you might call lectures in great meeting halls, or meet together to discuss ideas, and to learn from higher guides the nature of Earth life in terms of inner growth, and what needs to be done to achieve that in positive ways. It's especially jarring to leave Earth due to an accident, suicide, or murder. That is an unsettling experience, to say the least. Many challenging questions follow that kind of death.

All of these are major reasons why people return to a body after being in the etheric. The challenges—the really tough ones, that push you to grow in ways you never knew existed—tend to happen on Earth or other very dense, challenging planets. And there are things that can't be fully settled in the etheric. They need to be settled in an Earth life, where they began.

So you and a person you've had troubles with in any number of Earth lives will then meet up again, to work on resolving it this time. And of course, the same old interferences stick their noses in to complicate things, though that's another story.

## Now is the perfect time to admit your Divinity, and stop hiding it with the false modesty of the false self.

The spirit existence is not generally anywhere near as challenging, unless you are fulfilling a particular role that requires constant growth on your part. And even then—you're not in a dense body, but a much lighter, etheric one. You don't have to work out how to pay the rent and feed the children while you're doing the job. You're not subjected to illness and aging, and the fear that goes with that. And unless you choose to, you never feel you're alone.

Isolation is a human condition, though it can continue on, if the person is drawn to a sort of netherworld existence between dimensions, or to the lower dimensions, which I don't recommend.

In the higher realms, we support one another, without even thinking. It's automatic and fully integrated into our beings. It's the utopia I dreamed of while on Earth. Most people have experienced it, but to remember it while you're living in the density of the Earth plane would take some doing. Steady, deep meditation each day, a very refined set of life choices, and a highly committed spiritual path would lead you into it from time to time.

If you want to travel the higher realms and experience the Joy of it, you can. Just understand, as most people do, that you're not on the Earth to mainly live above it, so much as in it. That's not a picnic, to be down in the trenches, as you put it. Yet it's what you all wanted.

And now that the Earth is Ascending—moving up to a whole higher form of existence, where Peace and cooperation and open communication are the norm, where telepathy, compassion, higher technologies that heal and empower are the norm—now is the perfect time to admit your Divinity. To stop hiding it with the false modesty of the false self.

To return to your first question, I'm no longer sorry I'm not still on the Earth, because as I've said, I can do more from where I am at this time on Earth's timeline, than I could if I were a much older man, sounding irrelevant and worn out to most people. (Or still the angry activist.)

Millions are in the process of discovering there is no "age" situation really, just experience. People age in part because they expect to. But the Wisdom you desire can come whenever you call it forth. Just be careful: ask that it come to you in ways that are joyful, not challenging.

Believe me, hard-won wisdom is not an easy ride. There are happier ways!

# 12

# Souls and Spirits

*Over time I've come to realize what you mentioned earlier: that the soul is not always fully intact. That it suffers from our Earth lives.*

*A soul can be fragmented due to trauma from many lifetimes. It can hold an energy imprint from dark or dense experiences. Other situations are even worse than that.*

*I used to believe the soul was utterly indestructible. Yet it would stand to reason that it would suffer from its connection to our third dimensional lives, and its exposure to denser presences in this Universe.*

*Could you explain more?*

You've already hit upon a great deal, just by describing the things that can happen to a soul as humans (and other races of beings) journey through a physical life, as well as the dimensions.

This is because it is possible to be affected by what other groups or individuals do, even if your own intentions are very high, and your choices are very clear and high. There are beings in the Universe I would consider indestructible, but they are in the minority.

So there is a vulnerability for most on the soul level, as there is for the spirit, psyche, body. You could say that your spirit is the part of your consciousness that inhabits your Earth body, while your soul functions as the overseer of all your aspects. That is one interpretation—there are others.

Your higher self doesn't disappear when your spirit or your soul is fractured or fragmented in some way. But it is harder for your higher wisdom to guide a fractured being. This is why meditation and energy healing are so crucial.

So much of what you have experienced on the Earth is bigger than you. I don't recommend trying to fix it all on your own. You're too close to the issues to get a real, full view of them. And others—energy workers and healers with real skills—will not be so emotionally invested in your Earth life traumas as you are. They will be able to tell you what you experienced in this and other lives that you have not been fully aware of. That lets you know what's going on, on a level not really accessible by the conscious mind.

All you know is, you're suffering—you're depressed, or you've got insomnia, or none of your relationships seem to work, or you always expect to fail, or money disappears as fast it comes to you. Or you've got some anger that's always just below the surface, and you can't seem to work out what's caused it. I can guarantee you—you have no idea what you've been through, because Earth is such a dense place of utter forgetting.

A place for forgetting your true self, your Earth mission, your life experiences, over thousands or even millions of years. These are all a mystery, with clues popping up here and there, but no full picture revealed.

You and others have recommended to people that when they are squashed by some challenge, they get a pen and paper and write at the top, "Who are you, and why are you giving me such a hard time with _____ [name the issue]?" They then switch the pen to their nondominant hand, and let their subconscious write the answer.

What comes through might be a past life self, their child self, an ancestor, someone they knew in a past life. Or it might be a spirit or group of spirits who moved in long ago and decided to take over and steer that person's thoughts, personality, interests, words, and actions in the direction that *they* prefer. There are a number of possibilities. And without wanting to frighten or upset anyone, I would just say, unless you enjoy carrying these heavy inner (and outer) weights, invest some time and a bit of money in energy clearings, and stop dithering!

Yes, you have been affected by interferences. You're not immune. Almost no one is, while experiencing the extreme vulnerability of being in a human body.

*It is astounding, the number of interferences that can jump in and use our bodies, our life energies, our intentions, many of them not too friendly. And they can include beings as seemingly harmless as our ancestors. We like to assume they're always looking out for our higher good, but their outlook is often limited to what they believed at an earlier time on the Earth.*

*It's a huge issue, and one that people in the modern world in particular seem to be blind to.*

This is nothing new. It's more the modern world and pseudo-science that has considered that something doesn't exist until someone "discovers" it in a lab. And Western world religions decided it would take over and explain what happens to people spiritually, on Earth and in the "afterlife." For the most part, they've only succeeded at separating groups of people from one another and siphoning out their life energies, while failing humanity on so many levels.

**Humanity and the Earth have decided, right at the start of this new astrological cycle (the age of Aquarius), to begin again.**

You've heard that the reason the English call drink "spirits" is because centuries ago, those with clear inner sight could see or feel wandering spirits coming into pubs and gatherings, and these spirits (entities) loved nothing better than to move into the body of someone who was drunk or otherwise vacant from their body. These entities, who come from various places and dimensions, still hover in groups, in or above pubs, clubs, bars, parties—anywhere people gather to move into an altered state of lowered awareness, such as being drunk or high, or to support violence.

These entities feed off of the fractured mental noise and emotional desperation that drive so many to be in these places. The entities descend when the energies of a place or person open to the right (low) frequency for them to enter in and remain. Or when they spot a tear or opening in someone's aura, which might be from some trauma suffered at some point, or purely from being in an altered state—out of mind and body.

This isn't to say that all public drinking houses are automatically evil and low in frequency. We would just say, ask yourself how you feel about a place inwardly, before you enter. Try on its energy for a moment—imagine being inside those doors. Or just notice how you feel as you draw closer to the place or event.

Do you feel your energies going down? Staying the same? Rising a bit in a positive way, not an ego-high kind of way?

Pay attention, because the physical body reflects what the energetic body is picking up on, and clues you in with subtle or blatant shifts in breathing, or a tightened feeling in your gut, a tightening or releasing of muscles or of the throat, rapid blinking, or backing up a bit.

There are technological interferences as well. For one, be careful what films you watch, what music you listen to! Entertainment has its own matrix.

Your body, your mind and energies, are sacred space. You have to claim your sovereignty on your own. No one can do that for you. You can call in all kinds of energetic protection, but if you haven't made the strong determination that no one is allowed inside your body, mind, emotions, and energy bodies except you and your higher self—well, no one can make that decision for you. It awaits your command.

*Since it's unlikely that anyone ever becomes completely free of interferences while they're on the Earth, I'm wondering if there's something about being a human being that opens itself unknowingly to being used that way. Not an overt possession, but being used as a vessel for someone else's intentions.*

Unfortunately, humans are trained from birth to be a vessel for someone else's intentions. And I won't go into a lot of that, because I don't want anyone constantly glancing over their shoulder and wondering who is trying to run them. You still have a ton of self-determining free will that most people don't use or even know is there.

Let's just say you weren't created in your current form to serve your own dreams and visions. You were modified to serve what appears to be a corporate government structure, except it's more etheric and intergalactic than how you might image that.

What's interesting now is that humanity and the Earth have collectively decided, right at the start of this new 25,800-year astrological cycle (the age of Aquarius), to begin again. And this time they won't allow the downgrade. You'll oversee your own self-sufficiency. Run your own nations, institute your own higher principles and objectives, instead of being enslaved to someone else's destructive ones.

You'll Ascend to new heights in energy and awareness.

Humans are claiming their inner life and their own authority over their lives. They're valuing their own journey, their authenticity in ways that would not have occurred to anyone other than a few daring poets, visionaries, and dissidents in times past. This explains the crackdown on protests and demonstrations in the United States and elsewhere, with some places declaring them illegal, and seeking severe penalties for those participating.

But now, this amazing Light pouring in, which you're all responding to so powerfully, has made all the difference.

Though some people don't know why they're waking up to realizing the status quo is not good, not workable for the majority, and it's made them very uncomfortable. Because maybe they've been able to convince themselves over the years that even if the economic or political system in their country didn't work for everyone, it at least worked for them.

Now they're not so sure. They're seeing large cracks in the façade. That can shake people up.

Others have always been aware most of their lives, and are handling the news of what is going on in the world in ways that make it hard for them. Their sensitivity to energy and information has shot way up. Their reactions are based on survival training from maybe hundreds of past lives. They're wondering some days if humanity and other living beings will survive what's happening around them.

The anger that can result, or the feelings of hopelessness, could sink any ship. This is why it's critical that all aware and sensitive people take time not just to meditate but to spend time away from screens—away from information sources and all the energetic portals they contain. To spend time in Nature, connecting to Earth and absorbing her wisdom and presence.

It's vital that they do something to express themselves creatively as often as possible, whatever that is for them. And to spend time speaking with their higher self and spirit guides about anything that is troubling them about their path or what's happening on the Earth now.

Otherwise, it's easy to feel isolated and alone. It's easy to allow all the influences you've been taught to passively accept as real to run you and determine how you feel about life. And that kind of nonparticipation and victimhood, even if it feels natural and logical, is the last thing you're here for.

**_Does it help if we stop watching the news for the most part—especially social media, which can be so negative and alarmist?_**

Believe it or not, it helps tremendously to avoid all that, where you can. Because even a conscientious news broadcast that's being as honest as it is allowed to be, can be used to lower people's consciousness and vibration. So your refusal to participate with the lower energies transmitted there are crucial to your not being affected by it.

Really, from where we sit, if you would all spend your time concentrating on being joyful and doing what you love and encouraging others to do that, and stop focusing on what dreadful things might happen this year or next, *everything would improve.*

Your health and mental outlook would improve. You would eat less and enjoy it more, choosing more wisely what and how you ate, and when. Your emotional body would calm to where you would hardly recognize it anymore, that's how "Zen" and chilled you would be, come what may. Your relationships would improve because you would see your loved ones, coworkers, clients, everyone  as fellow travelers on the path, each with a unique presence, gifts, and insights of their own.

The negative judgments would stop. The angry complaints would stop. The feelings of loss, of being cheated by life, would end. Because you'd find that you and not some shadowy unseen figures somewhere had taken control of your day.

And that can make all the difference.

# 13

# A Sea of Energy

*Those who have come into Earth at this time to anchor Light into Earth and Earth systems, and into human life, are having as hard a time as anyone right now.*

*As this Light pours onto the planet, it seeks to heal us of all our old fragmentation and losses. All the old trauma and madness of human life. And for so many of us, there's a lot of density to clear.*

*Everything needing to be healed is rising to the surface now. There's all this emotion over unresolved issues. And the realization that just as surely as you or I have been mistreated and traumatized, we have mistreated others in one Earth life or another, and that too has to be cleared and released.*

*Do you have any words of encouragement for those at the bottom of the heap right now, in terms of how they're feeling about life? Because this is a lot to deal with at once.*

Yes, a very challenging time. Many have had a very hard time of it lately.

Not only those in a human body now, but those in Spirit are also experiencing great shifts, as their own dimensions increase in resonance and frequency. Nothing in this Universe ever remains the same. Humans may subconsciously think they've won the day with a stubborn outlook, not moving forward for great lengths of time, but even then, there's always change. There's always some form of renewal and rebirth of one's essence, or a degrading of it.

This is a time of accelerated Earth life processes. Instead of just moving forward spiritually here and there, you've moved into a sort of hyper-drive where everything seems haywire for a while, while you learn to view life on a whole other plane. And that means viewing the energy of each situation differently than how you'd have seen it in the past. Seeing every circumstance as an energy readout of what's happening within and without.

There's no sense asking things to return to how they were, because they can't. You notice how Time is moving so much faster now. You've calculated that an hour now passes in what used to be something like 15 minutes. That is correct. More like 12 minutes, actually.

Likewise, the average Light Bringer's speed of growth is now moving exponentially faster, so that what once passed for a year's worth of growth might happen in a month or less. That's not unusual.

***But it's too much for some people. Because while the energies may be requiring them to grow at an unprecedented, accelerated pace, their own mind and emotions may be only be able to deal with so much. And the pandemic and other tragedies have only made life even more stressful.***

And that's all the more reason for greater focus on your own needs and the demands of your path. Most people attend to spiritual practice as an afterthought or a daily ritual—doing the tapping or saying affirmations or a daily prayer, visualizing, meditating, yoga practice, etc.

All that is brilliant, but what you're all being called to now is much bigger than that. It's bigger than just talking to your higher self every now and again, or doing some spiritual practice because you're in hot water about something, and need answers.

It's more like you've been accelerated at school, five years ahead of where you were. And if you don't get serious and bear down on your studies, and make it an ongoing habit to stay conscious—to realize that you're in an energy mix, not just an outer situation—you will not only slow your own progress. You'll spiral into the lower emotional levels, as you say.

Understand that everything is energy, and begins there. The outer situation is just an outpicturing of that. None of what you're going through will make sense to you, until you view it as pure energy demonstration, and deal with it energetically.

### *I'm not sure most people know how to do that!*

They don't. That's why it's vital to learn how.

The first thing to realize is that any outer situation is a sort of hologram or metaphor for an inner situation. And the inner situation almost always begins in your heart and mind. The etheric, the world of energy, is mainly unseen on Earth at present, except for those meters that rate levels of sound or Light or density. Those are just *indications* of energy.

So that when you're walking down the street and see a homeless person and decide to give them some money or a sandwich, it's partly because you've picked up on their feeling displaced, hungry, and marginalized. That's why you give them something. Not just to make yourself feel better about their situation, but because you read in their energies that they're feeling abandoned by their family or culture, and it doesn't make sense that anyone should be abandoned to live alone on the streets.

You're not just feeding someone. You're sending them the message that they're not entirely alone or forgotten. If you stop and talk to them for a bit (if they are open to that), and ask if they have a shelter to go to at night, and if there's a food bank where they can get food regularly, you're then in a process of an energy exchange. They're sending you energy as you send them energy. They may be a very wise and high being, who came to Earth with the mission of being homeless at some point so that others like yourself could practice being compassionate and caring. That has happened many times. It's not unusual.

## You're not healing anyone by taking on their energy and losing your own.

So while you're helping them on a smaller level, they're helping you on a bigger level.

Now, there are other possibilities. It's possible that they have numerous energy interferences that have lowered their energies to where they can barely make sense of life. They may suffer from what is commonly called mental illness, which is rarely just that alone. If they are living on the street, it's doubtful they're getting the help they need. And the entities that inhabit them are making their lives extremely difficult.

So that when you stop to see if they're OK, they may snarl or yell or hide under a blanket and not want to interact with you. In that brief moment, you energetically pick up on what is happening with them, and even if you don't use technical phrases such as "entity attachments" and "energetic implants." And you're affected by it. You may unconsciously do a number of things.

You might send some of your life energy to this wounded being, to protect them from—you're not sure what—whatever seems to be assailing them from within. You might then carry on unconsciously working on them energetically, trying to free them from these interferences without even fully realizing you're doing that, for hours or even days after that. In the very least, you've taken on some of their trouble and turmoil, partly to save them from it, and partly because you relate to them in some way.

So now you've taken on energies that are not your own, and are carrying that density as if it was your own. You may have also given some of your life energy and strength to someone who never asked for it. They might consider both actions an imposition and an interference, and that is correct, even if it was compassion that spurred you on in the first place.

You don't want someone jumping into your life unbidden and working on solving your problems for you, and neither do they. Your own children, unless they're still fairly young, don't even want you to do that! No one seeking health and balanced, empowered well-being wants you to do that.

So why would you give away your own energies, which you so need to deal with your own challenges, and take on what isn't yours to carry?

"Because maybe part of why I'm here is to heal and encourage others," is what many would say. And that is great. But you're not healing anyone by taking on their energy and losing your own.

And why would you do that?

Because you are clueless as to how energy works—your own, and other people's. You think you can deposit and withdraw here and there, unconsciously and constantly, and that magically, that particular bank account won't ever run dry. Or it won't get filled up with bad currencies you have no use for, or that eat up the good currency.

I guess what I'm asking—what we're all asking of now—is that you all realize that you must become conscious of how your energy acts in any situation in your life, and understand that no outer situation just "happens." Everything you see is the result not just of thoughts, but of expectations. Of emotion, and the transfer of energy from thought and feeling to outer life.

If you look at your physical, financial bank balance and see not as much as you'd like to see, and you think, "I'm always out of money!"—guess what will happen, if you think that often enough? That very thing. Because the energy—the *command* you've sent to your bank account is one of loss and lack. And so it must follow orders.

Likewise, when you see the homeless person or even a loved one suffering, and you're not watching your thoughts and emotions in relation to them—you just let them flow unconsciously in an effort to solve their problem. When you connect in that way, you resonate with their situation, even if you would never want to experience that for yourself.

Perhaps on some level, you also feel to be abandoned and alone in life. In that case, the homeless person's situation would resonate with a feeling you already have.

So now you're not only trying to solve that person's sadness and isolation. You're trying to heal your own. But in resonating with that person's situation, you are matching it vibrationally. Even if you don't end up homeless yourself, some part of your experience will reflect the feeling of being displaced.

Or perhaps you feel a bit guilty, having a fairly abundant life while they have a hard life. In that case, giving away some of your energy to them, so they will feel better, is a way of apologizing for not experiencing poverty as they are.

In any event, you're somewhat leaning energetically out of your body as you speak to them. You're not viewing them from a detached place of objectivity and, in a sense, purity. You're asking them to feel better so *you* can feel better. Far better to keep a calm centeredness which respects the role and path they have chosen, and does not judge that as Good or Bad.

When you take on another's energy, you are slightly leaving your own body and flowing into their energies, and accepting them unconsciously. Carrying them as if they were your own. Which leaves you with far less mental, emotional, and physical energy with which to run your own life. And it leaves you carrying someone else's life energy, when you should only be carrying your own.

How could you possibly feel abundant and fulfilled, when you're carrying a homeless person's sense of displacement? That was never the point of meeting them. The point was that the homeless person's presence is helping you realize parts of your own being that feel lost and alone.

I don't say all this to discourage anyone from being compassionate! Of course you are here to help, to love and encourage others. My point, and the point many people's higher self and guides have been trying to make, is that the world's ills can't cost you your own life energies.

Your life is yours to run, to inhabit. The homeless person isn't going to do that for you. Your son or daughter who's hooked on drugs can't do that for you. That organization you just donated to can't do that for you. They can't experience for you the joy and fulfillment you came here to know.

You're the only one who can do that.

Let's go back to the subject of money for a moment.

Many, though not all of course, view money in a way that utterly reflects how they see their own life. As I said earlier, some will look at the balance in their account, and announce that it's "Not enough." That's interesting, because they tend to see their own life in much the same way. They don't feel they've *done* enough, generally. Haven't done enough for their child or their nephew or sister. Haven't done enough at work. Haven't worked hard enough at getting more fit and dropping more weight. Haven't saved the world from the evildoers, no matter how many petitions they've signed, demonstrations they've marched in, votes they've cast.

> **Every time you say to your money that it's not enough, you've *announced energetically to the Universe what's going to happen next.***

There's almost always a deficit. And so the spiritually sensitive person, tired of being accused by others or themselves as not being good enough, feels deflated and done in most days. They wander home after the work day and try to make up for that emptiness with a too-heavy meal that dulls the senses, or a few hours of telly or internet that distract them from the heaviness of unrelenting problems in the world. The feeling that too much has been left unsolved. Perhaps then a drink or two, or a good dose of sugar by way of an after-supper treat.

And that's all right. I'm not judging anyone for any of that. In my last life, I went in the opposite direction for years, trying *only* to please myself, and that doesn't work either, believe me!

Trouble is, if that's your life, you're not happy. And your guides and higher self keep nudging you to change things. Such as, to relax and revel in the beauty of nature as often as you can. To get away from screens as often as you can. To love and bless your body, your relationships, your bank accounts as always being *completely great* or *more than enough*. To stop saying "You've failed me" or "You never do enough" to the reflection in the mirror.

Every time you say to your money that it's not enough, or that it's more than enough, you are actively creating exactly what you say you are seeing. It's not just commentary. It's co-Creation. And you do that with how you *feel* when you look in your wallet, think about what you'd love to buy, or look at your savings, or how much you owe.

You've just *announced energetically to the Universe what's going to happen next*. And due to Universal law, it is bound to give you that. It has no choice but to give you some form of that.

It may take rereading this section and letting it sink in, because you've been programmed in the opposite belief your entire life, but if you're following this, you'll see how you live in a deficit of energy in many places in your life, not only in your bank accounts. This also affects your health, your love life. Any energy you carry as "truth" of how you're doing can easily spill into other areas, as it becomes your default position on whether life works for you or not, or whether the Universe seems to like you or not.

It's that way for everyone. It's not that you've done anything wrong. But you are in a time now when you must become aware of several things, on a near-constant basis. One of those things is being aware when you're giving your energy away instead of simply sending Light to someone in trouble. Calling on that person's higher self, spirit guides, and guardians, as well as your own support team, to assist them.

## Healing the entire planet won't make your own pain go away.

Another area is to become very aware when you're feeling low about your life in ways that say "Not enough" or "Not good enough" or "Cheated" or "Abandoned," or whatever refrain your subconscious keeps serving up.

None of that serves your higher good. It keeps you from experiencing it, while it's sitting right next to you, dying to be accepted.

I know that a lot of you are going to label these concepts as the law of attraction, or energy transference, or plenty of other phrases that are trending right now. I'm just going to call you back to the concept of self-Love and self-respect. Respect for the path you came in for.

And a lot of that has been painful. Because this particular Earth life is a final letting go point. You came in to heal the pain already experienced in other lives, and then to detach from those circumstances. *You are your first point of responsibility.* Healing the entire planet won't make your own pain go away.

But healing yourself while on the Earth plane has incredible power to it. And as you live out your own healing, you liberate millions of others to do the same.

You want to save the world? That's how you're doing to do it. Show them how it's done!

**So is your song "Imagine" not only about a fifth dimensional world, but also about imaging a life of fulfillment instead of being stuck in what we see around us right now?**

Well, that is the Ascension that "Imagine" referred to—using your imagination to pull out of your current circumstances energetically, and inwardly walk into the life and the world you would love to experience. I would have described it a little differently at the time. But that was the point of that song to a good degree.

As you visualize Peace, prosperity, calm, normalcy, you come out of the prescribed thinking you've been handed since childhood, in this and every life. You start visualizing a world that actually works, even in a pandemic.

A world where people work in concert with one another, not against one another. Where countries erase and dissolve their borders. Where the separations people and governments have thought so necessary for so long are no longer necessary. Where hatred and superstition are completely outmoded and healed. Where children and elders are respected, women held equal to men, and nonwhite held equal to white, and so on.

A world where no one is celebrating aggression and killing, or intimidation. No one is celebrating loss and sacrifice. No need for those war memorials anymore, because there's no need for war. No one is thinking, "We have to protect ourselves" against lack and scarcity, or against harsh weather, or an enemy, because those situations have been addressed with an understanding of how energy works. That it starts in our mental conceptions, and is spurred along into outer life by joyful emotion and positive expectation, and giving thanks.

And the way you do that is to have fun every day, imaging the beautiful things you would love to experience in your life, and for the world. Yes, imagine the crooks in the "seats of power" all over the world being escorted out in handcuffs, to face real justice. And yes, imagine all the crime syndicates likewise being broken up and their leaders and supporters arrested and made to face the reality of their crimes. (Same crowd, different day.)

But beyond that, use your co-creative power to imagine the Earth finally freed from all intrusions, all contaminations, all pollutants of any kind! Free of all invaders and intruders, all usurpers of free will choice.

Imagine the seas, lakes, rivers, streams sparking clean and speaking to humankind again (though they've never stopped), opening up the dialogue where they explain what they need from human beings, and what is harmful and hard for them. Imagine humans hearing them! And hearing the hills and mountains, the caves, the soil. Inner Earth as well as the planet's surface.

All life, all of Earth's elements, animals, insects speaking to all of humanity, as human beings hear and respond to them, so that the clash of interests that has been in place for thousands of years is no longer Earth's reality. All painful history, fading into the background as not only life-enhancing advanced technologies, but sovereign thought and social structures come into place.

In that Earth, there aren't so much governments, as wise councils such as one finds in the higher realms. There are courts of justice, but they serve the common person, not any elite power structure. There are forms of music, theatre, film. But they only exist to elevate thought and feeling. And there are forms of language, including telepathy, sign language, and symbolic languages, that erase international voids and gaps in understanding.

*It doesn't strike you that things have worsened with this pandemic? And as I write this, the worst wildfires California has yet seen?*

*Even once the virus finally dies out, our economy is gone. Millions are unemployed and without healthcare, and/or evicted or foreclosed on. So many are feeling not only lost, but desperate.*

Completely understandable that you would feel, looking at that outer situation, that this is a fall from normalcy and survival. Yet humanity will survive it, and you are.

What we who speak from the other side of life would offer you, is that things are never so out of control as they appear. Most of what people suffer now is not so much a matter of their current circumstances, but stress over what might happen next. What might happen to them next month or next year. What other losses might occur.

## *You* are the place of power now. Human consciousness is the most powerful thing on the planet.

From where I sit—and I multi-locate to different places on Earth, and to the ships—I see humanity stepping into a whole new role, in which you no longer look to those socially "above you" to lead the way. You have seen them floundering and lost, lying through their teeth and making huge errors in judgment, or carrying out orders designed to bring destruction.

You've seen them failing their own litmus tests on whether they can lead or not, as well as yours. And yet you still watch the news hoping for something positive to come from the old places of power.

Here's the interesting thing, and it's what I've been saying throughout: *You* are the place of power now. Human consciousness is the most powerful thing on the planet. Steeped in Light and higher intent, and capable of calling on the greatest allies this Universe has to offer, your consciousness is the path to the next level of thought and realization. To Peace, and to the fifth dimension.

This is why I say, *Heal yourself first!* Take care of your own health with proper healthy foods, quiet times, exercise, time in the natural world. One person doing this influences thousands of others to take their own health into their own hands. Don't label yourself as lost, or a potential victim waiting to fall prey to illness or panic over this issue or that. You determine your life at every moment.

There are already numerous powerful interventions taking place, in which the Angelic forces are moving steadily to assist humanity, where asked. You must ask, before anyone from the higher dimensions will assist. Unless they are fulfilling imperatives to which they were already committed, and you will not know what those are.

The whole idea of sovereignty is that *your free will is respected and honored*. We do not "rescue" for the same reason we do not seek to control humanity. And yet, yes—much help is at hand.

Call to you the wisdom to know what to do in any one situation. Keep your advisors—your guides and higher self, and all Angelic assistance—very close to you. Speak with them throughout the day. Ask them to assist you in staying grounded in the present moment, and picturing your higher good unfolding at every moment.

And yes, call in the Angelic forces, all forces of higher Light, to assist humanity and the Earth. The combined voices of millions—even of only a few—do not go unanswered! The timeline is moving so quickly, that I do not offer predictions, nor should anyone, if they are wise. Yet the higher outcome is clear, and you will not be regretting it.

An interesting thing, is that things had to get this difficult on the Earth before NESARA law would be fully enacted. All the wheels of co-Creation had to be moving in a particular way in order for NESARA's way to be paved. We see those mechanisms moving perfectly now. And even if all were progressing more slowly than it is, it would still progress.

You would still all be Ascending, if that is what you choose. And as your Collective say, you are never alone!

So many of the denser plans for Earth have failed, and will continue to do so.

### *You hold out hope for us then?*

I hold out more than hope, friend! I hold celebration! I hold out amazement that humanity has come so far in such a relatively short amount of time, though it won't seem that way to those on Earth now.

I would say, start celebrating what you know is inevitable now: the liberation of an entire planet. And you're here to see it!

This we know: that the way carved out from here to the higher realms is unfolding, and none of the powers of heaven and Earth can stop that now. All of you, as gods and goddesses who work with Universal energies to create the new, have decided that, and none can prevail against you.

I would just say, get off your seriousness! It's your job now to have a good laugh, to listen to music that inspires you, to stop feeling that the outer struggle around you defines your life. It doesn't.

Stop falling for appearances! Even the mountains you've been climbing are bowing to you now. The oceans, the rivers flow at your command. The skies await you. And you will get there.

Celebrate! Now is the time, friends.

And it's true—in all of this, you are never alone. And you are greatly loved.

# About the Author

Caroline Oceana Ryan is an author, channeler, speaker, and radio host. She has channeled information from Angels and spirit guides since childhood.

*Lennon Speaks* is her seventh book. She has channeled five books from the group of higher beings known as the Collective.

Ryan holds an MA in intercultural education and theological studies from Union Theological Seminary in New York City. She has published poetry in the United States, England, and Ireland. Her plays *A Witch's Cross* and *Rage Removers* were produced at the Sunset Gardner Stages in West Hollywood.

Visit www.CarolineOceanaRyan.com (or AscensionTimes. com) to sign up for the weekly "Message to Lightworkers" channelings, and for information on channeling sessions, the Abundance Group, and guided meditations by the Collective.

# Other Books by Caroline Oceana Ryan

**The Fifth Dimensional Life series (channeled from the Collective):**

*Abundance For All: The Lightworker's Way to Creating Money and True Wealth* (2016)

*Connections: The Collective Speak on Romance and Friendship* (2017)

*Earth Life Challenges: The Collective Speak on Dealing with Trauma and Life Changes* (2018)

**The Ascension Manual series (channeled from the Collective):**

*The Ascension Manual – Part One: A Lightworker's Guide to Fifth Dimensional Living* (2015)

*The Ascension Manual – Part Two: Creating a Fifth Dimensional Life* (2016)

**Also by Caroline Oceana Ryan**

*Adventures in Belfast: Northern Irish Life After the Peace Agreement* (2014)

## Available on Amazon

Printed in Great Britain
by Amazon